Scott Foresman - Addison Wesley
MATH

Technology Masters
Grade 5

Scott Foresman - Addison Wesley

Editorial Offices: Menlo Park, California • Glenview, Illinois
Sales Offices: Reading, Massachusetts • Atlanta, Georgia • Glenview, Illinois
Carrollton, Texas • Menlo Park, California

http://www.sf.aw.com

ISBN 0-201-31306-5

Copyright © Addison Wesley Longman, Inc.

All rights reserved. The blackline masters in this publication are designed to be used with appropriate equipment to reproduce copies for classroom use only. Addison Wesley Longman grants permission to classroom teachers to reproduce these masters.

Printed in the United States of America

6 7 8 9 10 – BW – 02 01 00

Technology Table of Contents

Overview ... iv

1: Using a Calculator to Solve Problems: Choose the Operation ... 1
2: Using a Calculator to Explore Algebra ... 2
3: Using a Calculator to Solve Line Graph Problems ... 3
4: Using a Computer to Make a Graph ... 4
5: Using a Calculator to Explore Place Value through Millions ... 5
6: Using a Calculator to Explore Place-Value Relationships ... 6
7: Using a Computer to Compare and Order Numbers ... 7
8: Using a Calculator to Explore Thousandths ... 8
9: Using a Calculator to Round Decimals ... 9
10: Using a Calculator to Add Whole Numbers ... 10
11: Using a Calculator to Add and Subtract Decimals ... 11
12: Using a Calculator to Explore Place-Value Relationships ... 12
13: Using a Calculator to Find Multiples of Numbers ... 13
14: Using a Calculator to Perform Order of Operations ... 14
15: Using a Calculator to Solve Multiple-Step Problems ... 15
16: Using a Calculator to Multiply Decimals ... 16
17: Using a Calculator to Estimate Quotients and Remainders ... 17
18: Using a Calculator to Divide with 1-Digit Numbers ... 18
19: Using a Calculator to Divide Money ... 19
20: Using a Calculator to Divide Greater Numbers ... 20
21: Using a Calculator to Find the Mean ... 21
22: Using a Computer to Explore Quadrilaterals ... 22
23: Using a Calculator to Simplify Fractions ... 23
24: Using a Calculator to Compare and Order Fractions ... 24
25: Using a Calculator to Convert Improper Fractions to Mixed Numbers ... 25
26: Using a Calculator to Connect Fractions, Decimals, and Percents ... 26
27: Using a Calculator to Find the Least Common Denominator ... 27
28: Using a Calculator to Add Fractions and Mixed Numbers ... 28
29: Using a Calculator to Explore Feet, Yards, and Miles ... 29
30: Using a Calculator to Find the Products of Fractions, Mixed Numbers, and Whole Numbers ... 30
31: Using a Calculator to Multiply Whole Numbers by Fractions ... 31
32: Using a Calculator to Multiply Whole Numbers and Mixed Numbers ... 32
33: Using a Calculator to Find the Perimeters of Polygons ... 33
34: Using a Calculator to Find the Perimeters of Rectangles ... 34
35: Using a Calculator to Convert Units to Find Perimeter ... 35
36: Using a Calculator to Find the Area of Rectangles ... 36
37: Using a Calculator to Find the Area of Triangles ... 37
38: Using a Calculator to Find the Area of Parallelograms ... 38
39: Using a Calculator to Explore Circumference ... 39
40: Using a Calculator to Find Surface Area ... 40
41: Using a Calculator to Explore Ounces, Pounds, and Tons ... 41
42: Using a Calculator to Find Volume ... 42
43: Using a Calculator to Find Measurements for a Scale Drawing ... 43
44: Using a Calculator to Find the Percent of a Number ... 44

Overview

IMPORTANCE OF USING TECHNOLOGY

NCTM Recommendations

The use of technology at all grade levels has become an integral part of teaching and learning mathematics. Since the early 1980s, the National Council of Teachers of Mathematics (NCTM) has consistently held a strong, positive position on the use of calculators and computers in mathematics learning. More recently, the NCTM has reaffirmed this position through its "Standards" publications (i.e., *Curriculum Standards*, *Assessment Standards*, and *Professional Standards*) and through its issuance, and re-issuance, of two position statements: *Calculators and the Education of Youth (February 1991)* and *The Use of Technology in the Learning and Teaching of Mathematics (February 1994)*.

The use of calculators in students' everyday lives continues to grow. Thus, it is easy to understand why the NCTM's position statement concerning their use (February 1991) recommends "… the integration of the calculator into the school mathematics program at all grade levels in classwork, homework, and evaluation." (page 18, NCTM 1996–97 Handbook) The need for students to be well-versed in the appropriate use of calculators is even more striking when one thinks about the continual explosion of mathematics in our technological world. Indeed, "… increased use of calculators in school will ensure that students' experiences in mathematics will match the realities of everyday life, develop their reasoning skills, and promote the understanding and application of mathematics." (page 18, NCTM 1996–97 Handbook)

Clearly, the successful student of the 21st century will have a working knowledge of mathematics solidly coupled with a clear understanding of the appropriate use of calculator technology. The importance of good mathematics instruction then becomes even clearer since "instruction with calculators will extend the understanding of mathematics and will allow all students access to rich, problem-solving experiences." (page 18, NCTM 1996–97 Handbook) It is just as clear that "instruction must develop students' abilities to know how and when to use a calculator." (page 18, NCTM 1996–97 Handbook) Indeed, good mathematics teaching must include the use of these powerful tools in an ongoing, well-developed mathematics program. This is why NCTM recommends "… that every mathematics teacher at every level promote the use of calculators to enhance mathematics instruction by modeling the use of calculators in a variety of situations." (page 18, NCTM 1996–97 Handbook)

However, simply teaching with these tools is not enough. Since students will use calculators as facilitators of their mathematics learning, it will be incumbent upon teachers to understand that "evaluation must be in alignment with normal, everyday use of calculators in the classroom." (page 18, NCTM 1996–97 Handbook) If this is not the case, then students will not learn the appropriate use of this technology.

Students who learn to use these tools for thinking will have a richer mathematics background since those who use calculators will be able to "… explore and experiment with mathematical ideas such as patterns, numerical and algebraic properties, and functions." (page 18, NCTM 1996–97 Handbook) To deny such a background to students is to deny them future opportunities that involve mathematical thinking.

Finally, the NCTM position statement on the use of calculators ends with the following: "Research and experience have clearly demonstrated the potential of calculators to enhance students' learning in mathematics… The calculator is an essential tool for all students of mathematics."

Furthermore, technology in general must find its way into the mathematics classroom. These tools include "… computers, appropriate calculators (scientific, graphing, programmable, etc.), videodisks, CD-ROM, telecommunications networks by which to access and share real-time data, and other emerging educational technologies." (page 24, *The Use of Technology in the Learning and Teaching of Mathematics*, NCTM 1996–97 Handbook) Teachers teaching with technological tools must become commonplace as we continue to move into a technologically-rich world. Indeed, NCTM strongly advocates the use of technology in the mathematics classroom: "Every student is to have access to a calculator appropriate to his or her level. Every classroom where mathematics is taught should have at least one computer for demonstrations, data acquisition, and other student use at all times." (page 24, NCTM 1996–97 Handbook)

Research Recommendations
Although advances in the development of technological teaching tools seem to have made teaching mathematics easier, the truth of the matter is that such advances have further complicated the lives of mathematics teachers. The calculator and computer explosion has provided teachers with an arsenal of incredible teaching and learning tools while, at the same time, causing considerable strain on their attempts to stay technologically current. Indeed, as Jensen and Williams[1] state, both teachers and researchers have found that technology does not necessarily offer all the answers. However, Jensen and Williams go on to point out that it is clear from research that the skillful use of computers and calculators increases the number of ways teachers can deliver content that has traditionally been difficult for middle grade students.

The fear of students not learning mathematics due to calculator use is unfounded. Study after study has shown that students who have been taught the appropriate use of calculators encounter no difficulties when performing paper-and-pencil computations. However, student attitudes toward mathematics and achievement in problem-solving have been positively affected by the appropriate use of calculators in mathematics.[2] The use of computers and calculators offers students the opportunity to experience mathematics in a variety of representational settings. Students can use these tools to explore patterns, make conjectures, and solve problems. Research has clearly demonstrated the powerful, positive effects of calculator and computer usage on critical thinking skills.

Jensen and Williams (page 239) also have provided some helpful hints to assist teachers who use technology in the classroom: (1) Provide students with clear directions, both orally and in writing, for the use of any software; (2) Make sure students are aware of, and can carry out, procedures for basic use of computers; (3) Develop a standard for behavior during technology lessons, including a method for getting the attention of the teacher; and (4) Develop an equal-access method for students to use the technology.

TECHNOLOGY MASTERS

The technology masters you will find in this book have been developed to provide students with opportunities to learn how to use technology in a meaningful way. The use of these masters will aid students' understanding of the technology used as well as solidify their understanding of the mathematical concept or skill. Students will find that completing the technology masters will increase their understanding of the mathematics presented in the specific lesson.

Research has shown that technology can provide a positive influence on attitudes as well as understanding in mathematics classes. The NCTM position statement on the use of technology (February 1994) indicates that "the use of the tools of technology is integral to the learning and teaching of mathematics. Students are to learn how to use technology as a tool for processing information, visualizing and solving problems, exploring and testing conjectures, accessing data, and verifying their solutions."

Calculator Masters
The calculator masters for Grade 5 all assume students are using a Math Explorer or its equivalent. Keystrokes are provided for the Math Explorer; however, most of the masters could be completed using any fraction-capable calculator.

DataWonder! and ClarisWorks Masters
Each of the technology masters that involves making a table or graphing has been written for DataWonder! or ClarisWorks. However,

these masters could easily be completed using any spreadsheet software with minor alterations in keystrokes or steps.

HOW TO USE THE TECHNOLOGY MASTERS

Each technology master is keyed to a specific student page or pages within a given chapter, and will reinforce the mathematical content as well as the use of a specific technology.

When a technology master is keyed to a specific page, the content of the master is the same as that on the student page and provides an alternate way of completing the task or activity.

Technology masters that are keyed to a sequence of pages in a chapter are connected to the concepts developed in that Lesson and provide students with an opportunity to solidify their understanding of the mathematics topics presented. Sometimes this is done by focusing on a specific strategy, sometimes by focusing on the development of a concept, and sometimes by focusing on a specific capability of the technology.

Each technology master has been written with the assumption that the technology itself should not get in the way of meaningful mathematics learning. Thus, each master provides detailed step-by-step instructions for the use of the required technology so as to allow students to focus on the mathematics rather than the implementation of the technology. By allowing students to work through these technology masters, they will not only gain an appreciation of the power and usefulness of technology, but more importantly, they will increase their mathematical power.

[1] Jensen, R. J. and Williams, B. (1993) Technology: Implications for Middle Grades Mathematics. In D. T. Owens (Ed.), *Research Ideas for the Classroom: Middle Grades Mathematics* (pp. 225–241). New York, NY: Macmillan Publishing Company.

[2] Hembree, R., and Dessart, D. J. (1986). Effects of Hand-Held Calculators in Precollege Mathematics: A Meta-Analysis. *Journal for Research in Mathematics Education*, 17(2), 83–99.

Name _____

Technology Master 1

Using a Calculator to Solve Problems: Choose the Operation

Suggested Technology: Calculator—Math Explorer or equivalent

This bar graph shows how much money 4 high school students earned during the summer for 1 month. How much more money did Kayla earn than Cody?

The graph shows that Kayla earned $90 and Cody earned $30.

Press [ON/C]

Press 9 0 [−] 3 0 [=]

Display shows: | 60. |

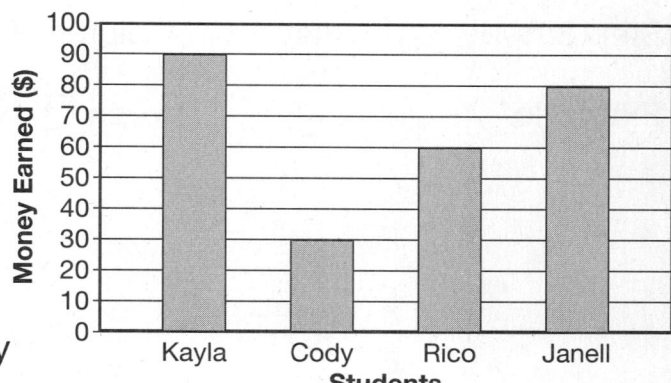

Since this problem involves money amounts, the answer is $60.

Kayla earned $60 more than Cody.

Use your calculator and the bar graph above to solve each problem. First read the problem and choose the operation. Show the keys to press and what the display will show. Then label each answer.

	Press	Display	Answer
1. How much money did Rico and Cody earn in 1 month?	_____	_____	_____
2. How much money will Cody earn at this rate in 3 months?	_____	_____	_____
3. If Janell is paid $5 an hour, how many hours did she work?	_____	_____	_____

4. Make up your own problem using the information from the bar graph. Have a classmate use a calculator to solve the problem.

_____

Name _____

Technology Master 2

Using a Calculator to Explore Algebra

Suggested Technology: Calculator—Math Explorer or equivalent

You can use the [Cons] key to complete T tables by following these steps:

Step 1: Press the rule and the [Cons] key.

Step 2: Press each number in Column A followed by the [Cons].

Step 3: Write each display in Column B.

Example Rule: $n \times 3$ **Press** [X] 3 [Cons]

A	B
2	6
5	15
6	18

Press	Display
2 [Cons]	6.
5 [Cons]	15.
6 [Cons]	18.

[CE/C] to clear

Use the [Cons] key to complete each T table. Write the keys you will press for the first two tables.

1. Rule: $n \times 8$ **Press** [X] 8 [Cons]

A	B	Press	Display
12	___	___	___
32	___	___	___
61	___	___	___
13	___	___	___

2. Rule: $n \div 7$ **Press** [÷] 7 [Cons]

A	B	Press	Display
91	___	___	___
84	___	___	___
63	___	___	___
133	___	___	___

3. Rule: $n + 12$

A	B
23	___
37	___
76	___
44	___

4. Rule: $n - 29$

A	B
94	___
81	___
41	___
68	___

5. Rule: $n - 4$

A	B
10	___
15	___
20	___
25	___

Name _____

Technology Master 3

Using a Calculator to Solve Line Graph Problems

Suggested Technology: Calculator—Math Explorer or equivalent

This line graph shows the number of cars sold by one car dealership in a 12-month period. How many cars were sold in all from January through March?

The graph shows that in January 50 cars were sold, in February 60 were sold, and in March 55 were sold.

Press [ON/C] then

Press 5 0 [+] 6 0 [+] 5 5 [=]

Display shows: *165.* 165 cars were sold in all from January through March.

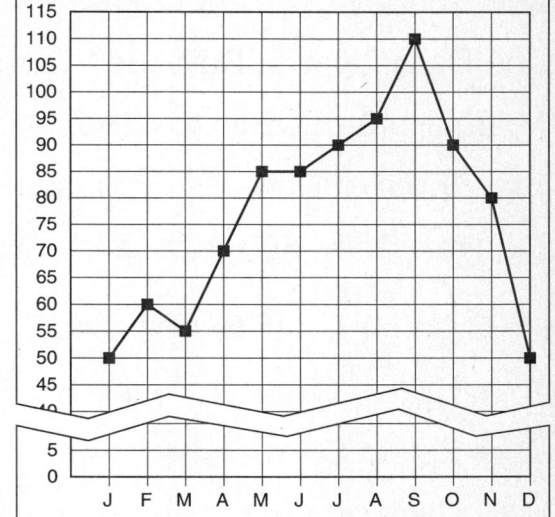

Use your calculator and the line graph above to solve each problem. Show the keys to press, the display, and your answer.

Press **Display** **Answer**

1. How many more cars were sold in September than in April? _____ _____ _____

2. How many more cars were sold in September than in December and January combined? _____ _____ _____

3. If the same number of cars were sold each of 4 weeks in February, how many cars were sold each week? _____ _____ _____

4. Make up a problem based on the line graph above. Have a classmate use a calculator to solve it.

_____

Name _____

Technology Master 4

Using a Computer to Make a Graph

Suggested Technology: Spreadsheet—ClarisWorks or equivalent

A group of fifth graders found the following information about the daily and Sunday circulation of 5 newspapers:

The Dallas News: Daily–504 thousand; Sunday–834 thousand

Miami Herald: Daily–414 thousand; Sunday–543 thousand

Star-Tribune: Daily–414 thousand; Sunday–696 thousand

Inquirer: Daily–503 thousand; Sunday–965

A. Create a table for the data.

- Choose **New** from the **FILE** menu.
- Select **Spreadsheet**, then click **OK.**
- Click on the rows and columns of the table as you complete the information as shown below:

	Newspapers	Daily	Sunday
1	Dallas	504	834
2	Miami	414	543
3	Star	414	696
4	Inquirer	503	965

B. Make a graph of the data.

- Highlight all of the cells in the table.
- Choose **Make Chart** from the **OPTIONS** menu.
- Look at all the graphs. Click on your choice of graph.
- Click on **Labels**, then enter a new title for your graph. Click **OK.**

Use the table and the graph to answer these questions.

1. Which newspaper has the greatest circulation? _____

2. Which newspaper has the lowest? _____

3. Are daily or Sunday circulations higher in general? _____

4 Use with pages 40–41.

Name _____

Technology Master 5

Using the Calculator to Explore Place Value through Millions

Suggested Technology: Calculator—Math Explorer or equivalent

You can use your calculator to add or subtract numbers written in word form.

Example:	**Press:**	**Display:**
Four hundred fifty-two thousand, one hundred thirty-five **plus** five hundred forty-seven thousand, eight hundred sixty-five.	[4][5][2][1][3][5][+] [5][4][7][8][6][5][=]	1000000

The answer with commas is 1,000,000.

Complete the following using your calculator. Put commas in the Displays.   **Press:**   **Display:**

1. Two million, eight hundred thousand **minus** one million, seven hundred thousand. _____ _____

2. Eight hundred forty-six thousand, thirty-eight **plus** fifty-three thousand, nine hundred sixty-two. _____ _____

3. Six million four hundred thousand, five hundred **minus** five million five hundred ninety-nine thousand, seven hundred. _____ _____

4. Seven hundred eighty-nine thousand, three hundred **plus** two hundred one thousand, six hundred nine. _____ _____

5. One million, one hundred one thousand, one **minus** two hundred twenty thousand, nine hundred ninety-three. _____ _____

6. How did you decide where to place your commas? _____

Name _____

Technology Master 6

Using a Calculator to Explore Place-Value Relationships

Suggested Technology: Calculator—Math Explorer or equivalent

You can use a calculator to find the values for greater factors of 10. Use the [×] and [=] keys to complete the pattern.

Factors of 10	Press	Display	Number name
10	1[×]10[=]	10	ten
10×10	1[×]10[=][=]	100	one hundred
10×10×10	_____	_____	_____
10×10×10×10	_____	_____	_____
10×10×10×10×10	_____	_____	_____
10×10×10×10×10×10	_____	_____	_____

What pattern do you see? _____

_____

How many factors of 10 can you use your calculator to find the value for?

Why? _____

You can use a calculator to find the value of 10 in exponent forms. Use the [10ⁿ] key and the number of the exponent to complete the pattern.

Exponent form	Press	Display	Number name
10^1	[10ⁿ] 1	10	ten
10^2	_____	_____	_____
10^3	_____	_____	_____
10^4	_____	_____	_____
10^5	_____	_____	_____
10^6	_____	_____	_____

What pattern do you see? _____

What is the greatest power of 10 you can evaluate using your calculator?

Why _____

6 Use with pages 56–57.

Name _____

Technology Master 7

Using a Computer to Compare and Order Numbers

Suggested Technology: Spreadsheet—ClarisWorks or equivalent

You can use your computer to compare the population of some states in 1950 with their population in 1990.

A. Create a table for your data. Choose **New** from the **FILE** menu. Select **Spreadsheet**, then click **OK**.

1. Click on the rows and columns of the table and fill in the information.

	A	B	C
1	States	1950	1990
2	Alaska	129,000	550,000
3	Delaware	318,000	636,000
4	North Dakota	620,000	639,000
5	South Dakota	653,000	696,000
6	Vermont	378,000	563,000
7	Wyoming	291,000	454,000

B. Highlight all of the cells in the table. Choose **Make Chart** from the **OPTIONS** menu. Look at the different graphs available. Choose the one you think best shows the data. Click on **Labels**, then enter a new title for the graph. Click on **General** and click on the box next to the **First Row**. Click **OK**.

2. Which graph did you choose? Explain. _____

_____

3. Which state's population doubled from 1950 to 1990? _____

4. Which state's population was about four times more in 1990 than in 1950? _____

5. Which states had more people in 1950 than either Alaska, Vermont, or Wyoming had in 1990? _____

6. Write the states in order from least to greatest population in 1950.

_____

_____

Use with pages 60–61. **7**

Name _____

Technology Master 8

Using the Calculator to Explore Thousandths

Suggested Technology: Calculator—Math Explorer or equivalent

You can use your calculator to play "Wipe Out."

- Enter a decimal number that has tenths, hundredths, and thousandths. Make each digit different. Do not use zero.
- Use addition or subtraction to change the "Wipe Out" number to zero.

Example: The number is 26.413. The "Wipe Out" number is 3.

Use subtraction.

Press [2][6][.][4][1][3]

Display 26.413

Press [−][0][.][0][0][3][=]

Display 26.41

Or use addition.

Press [2][6][.][4][1][3]

Display 26.413

Press [+][0][.][0][0][7][=]

Display 26.42

Now try these.

	Decimal Number	"Wipe Out Number"	Your Method
1.	23.976	9	
2.	456.789	5	
3.	3.842	4	
4.	12.953	3	
5.	2.385	2	
6.	382.671	1	

7. What conclusion can you make about the two numbers that can wipe out a digit? _____

8. Make up your own "Wipe Out" example. Choose a decimal number. Choose a digit to wipe out. Have a friend solve it.

_____

Use with pages 70–71.

Name _____

Technology Master 9

Using a Calculator to Round Decimals

Suggested Technology: Calculator—Math Explorer or equivalent

You can use the [FIX] key to round decimals. Press [FIX] 1 to round to the nearest tenth (1 decimal place), or [FIX] 2 to round to the nearest hundredth (2 decimal places) and then enter the number to be rounded.

Example 1: Round 0.378 to the nearest tenth.

Press	Display
[FIX] [1] [.] [3] [7] [8] [=]	0.4

Press [FIX] 2 to round to the nearest hundredth (2 decimal places).

Example 2: Round 0.378 to the nearest hundredth.

Press	Display
[FIX] [2] [.] [3] [7] [8] [=]	0.38

Use the [FIX] key to complete the following table.

Decimal Number	Rounded to the nearest tenth	Rounded to the nearest hundredth
1. 0.6753	_____	_____
2. 2.563	_____	_____
3. 3.0865	_____	_____
4. 12.782	_____	_____
5. 0.00876	_____	_____
6. 0.123	_____	_____
7. 5.5555	_____	_____

Explore

8. How do you think you could use your calculator to round a decimal to the nearest thousandth? _____

9. Use your method to round 1.8769 to the nearest thousandth.

_____

10. Did your method work? How can you tell?

_____

_____

Use with pages 76–77.

Name _____

Technology Master 10

Using the Calculator to Add Whole Numbers

Suggested Technology: Calculator—Math Explorer or equivalent

Use the distances on the U. S. map and your calculator to find the total distance traveled. The first one is done for you.

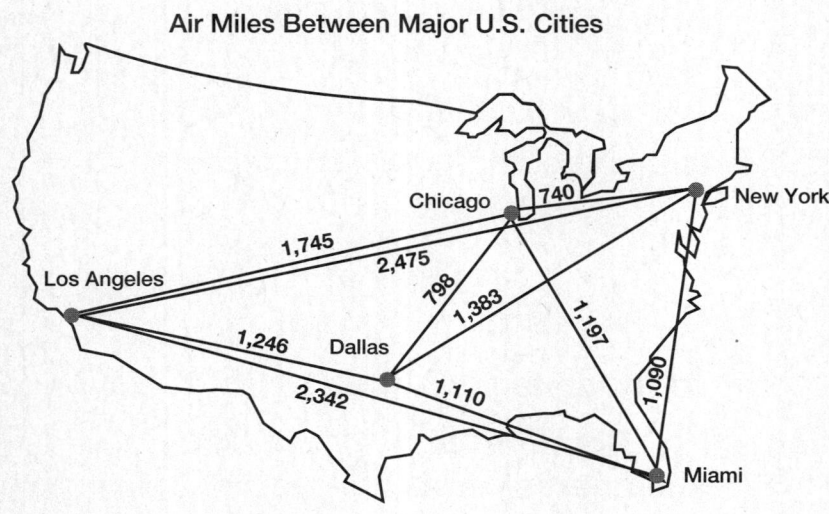
Air Miles Between Major U.S. Cities

Total Distance

1. Los Angeles to Chicago to New York City

   Press [1][7][4][5][+][7][4][0][=]   2,485 mi

2. New York City to Miami to Los Angeles to Chicago

   Press [1][0][9][0][+][2][3][4][2][+][1][7][4][5][=]   _____

3. Round trip between Los Angeles and New York City

   Press [2][4][7][5][+][2][4][7][5][=]   _____

4. Round trip between Dallas and Chicago.

   Press [7][9][8][+][7][9][8][=]   _____

5. Suppose you could earn a free trip by traveling a total of 25,000 miles. What trips would you take to earn the free trip (if you live in Miami)?

   _____

   _____

10 Use with pages 84–87.

Name _____

Technology Master 11

Using the Calculator to Add and Subtract Decimals

Suggested Technology: Calculator—Math Explorer or equivalent

Use your calculator to find the missing numbers in these magic squares. In a magic square, the sum is the same for the numbers in each row, column, and diagonal.

Here's how to find the first missing number:

Press [7][.][7][4][−][3][.][3][9][−][2][.][8][5][=] **Display** 1.5

Use this strategy to find the rest.

Magic Sum: 7.74

3.39	1.5	2.85
		1.77

Magic Sum: 5.6

2.6	0.7	1.2	
	1.8		2
0.8		1	
1.7			0.2

Magic Sum: 3.9

0.66		1.5	0.12	
0.6		1.14		0.18
			1.2	1.32
1.38		0.42	0.84	0.96
		0.06	0.48	0.9

What strategy did you use to find the missing numbers?

_____

_____

_____

Name

Technology Master 12

Using the Calculator to Explore Place Value Relationships

Suggested Technology: Calculator—Math Explorer or equivalent

Use the ⨯ and = keys to find the largest possible product for each set of digits. The first is done for you.

1. Make the greatest product. Use digits 2, 7, 9.

   ```
    7 2
   ×  9
   ―――
     648
   ```

Press	Display
27 × 9 =	243
92 × 7 =	644
72 × 9 =	648

2. Make the least product. Use digits 2, 7, 9.

   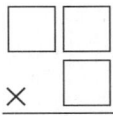

3. Make the greatest product of a 1-digit and a 3-digit number. Use digits 1, 3, 4, 8.

   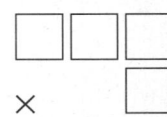

4. Make the least product of a 1-digit and a 3-digit number. Use digits 1, 3, 4, 8.

5. Make the greatest product of two 2-digit numbers. Use digits 1, 3, 4, 8.

   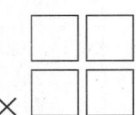

6. Make the least product of two 2-digit numbers. Use digits 1, 3, 4, 8.

   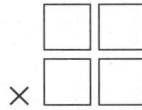

7. Make the greatest product of a 2-digit and a 3-digit number. Use digits 5, 6, 7, 8, 9.

   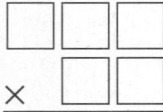

8. Make the least product of a 2-digit and a 3-digit number. Use digits 5, 6, 7, 8, 9.

   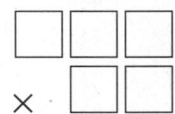

Name _____

Technology Master 13

Using a Calculator to Find Multiples of Numbers

Suggested Technology: Calculator—Math Explorer or equivalent

You can use the ⌗=⌘ key on your calculator to find the least common multiple (LCM) of two or more numbers.

Examples:

Numbers	Press = at least 5 times	Display	LCM
8	+8 = = = = =	8, 16, 24, 32, ㊵	
10	+10 = = = = =	10, 20, 30, ㊵, 50	40

40 is the least common multiple of 8 and 10.

Note: If there is no common multiple to either number after pressing the = key 5 times, press the = key several more times for each number.

Use a calculator to find the LCM for each set of numbers.

	Numbers	Press =	Display	LCM
1.	6	_____	_____	
	8	_____	_____	_____
2.	8	_____	_____	
	12	_____	_____	_____
3.	5	_____	_____	
	9	_____	_____	
	15	_____	_____	_____
4.	4	_____	_____	
	5	_____	_____	
	10	_____	_____	_____

Use with pages 126–127.

Name _____

Technology Master 14

Using a Calculator to Perform Order of Operations

Suggested Technology: Calculator—Math Explorer or equivalent

You can use two different methods on a calculator to solve problems using the order of operations.

Example: Solve using the order of operations: (7 + 8) − (12 ÷ 4).

Method 1:
Use ⌈(⌉ and ⌈)⌉ keys

Press	Display
⌈(⌉ 7 ⌈+⌉ 8 ⌈)⌉ ⌈−⌉ ⌈(⌉ 12 ⌈÷⌉ 4 ⌈)⌉ ⌈=⌉	12

When you use these keys just input the numbers and ( ) in the order they are in. The calculator does the math in the correct order.

Method 2:
Use ⌈M+⌉, ⌈M−⌉, and ⌈MR⌉ keys.

Press	Display
7 ⌈+⌉ 8 ⌈=⌉ ⌈M+⌉ 12 ⌈÷⌉ 4 ⌈=⌉ ⌈M−⌉ ⌈MR⌉	12

The ⌈M+⌉ key saves 7 + 8 in memory. The ⌈M−⌉ key subtracts 12 ÷ 4 from the first amount. The ⌈MR⌉ key shows the results.

Use both methods on your calculator to solve each problem. Write the keys you press for each method and the display.

	Method 1: ⌈(⌉ ⌈)⌉ Press	Display	Method 2: ⌈M+⌉, ⌈M−⌉, ⌈MR⌉ Press	Display
1. (14 × 6) − (5 × 6)				
2. 52 − (12 ÷ 3 × 2)				
3. (18 − 3) + (6 × 5 ÷ 2)				
4. 75 + (32 ÷ 4 + 6)				
5. (76 − 32 ÷ 4) − 60				

6. Which method did you prefer? Why?

_____

14 Use with pages 130–131.

Name _____

Technology Master 15

Using a Calculator to Solve Multiple-Step Problems

Suggested Technology: Calculator—Math Explorer or equivalent

You can use the (and) keys or the M+ and MR keys to solve multiple-step problems.

Delicious Deli Delights					
Potato Salad $1.25/lb	Turkey Bologna $1.99/lb	Honey Roast Ham $3.99/lb	Smoked Turkey $4.35/lb	Lovely Liverwurst $3.59/lb	Provolone Cheese $3.79/lb

Example: How much would you pay for:

	Press using M+ and MR keys.	Display	Solution
3 lb potato salad	3 × 1.25 = M+	3.75	
1 lb cheese	3.79 M+	3.79	
2 lb ham	2 × 3.99 = M+	7.98	
	MR	15.52	$15.52
Using parentheses.	(3 × 1.25) + 3.79 + (2 × 3.99) =	15.52	$15.52

Find the cost.

Press using M+ and MR keys.   Display   Solution

1. 3 lb smoked turkey _____ _____

  1 lb liverwurst _____ _____

  2 lb cheese _____ _____ _____

  Using parentheses _____

  _____ _____ _____

2. 5 lb bologna _____ _____

  2 lb potato salad _____ _____ _____

  Using parentheses _____

  _____ _____ _____

Use with pages 140–141.

Using the Calculator to Multiply Decimals

Suggested Technology: Calculator—Math Explorer or equivalent

It is useful to estimate a product when you use a calculator just in case you press a wrong key or forget a number.

Make an estimate for each problem. Then find the decimal product. Use the ⋅ key.

Hint: Look at the whole number parts of the problem.

	Problem	Estimate	Product	Close	Not close
1.	Example: 4 × 3.92	4 × 4 = 16	Press: 4 × 3.92 = Display: 15.68	✓	
2.	2.1 × 79				
3.	3.9 × 1.2				
4.	5.09 × 88				
5.	82.0 × 9.0				
6.	64 × 0.9				
7.	0.4 × 0.79				
8.	40 × 0.19				
9.	320 × 0.49				
10.	6.832 × 9.075				

How close were your estimates to the actual product?
Mark "Close" or "Not close" in the chart.

Name _____

Technology Master 17

Using a Calculator to Estimate Quotients and Remainders

Suggested Technology: Calculator—Math Explorer or equivalent

Use **compatible numbers** to estimate a quotient. Then use the [INT÷] key to find the exact quotient.

Examples: **Estimate quotient.**   Use [÷] **key to find quotient.**   Exact Quotient

Press   Display   Press   Display

248 ÷ 5 ≈   250 [÷] 5 = 50   248 [INT÷] 5 = $_Q$ 49 $_R$ 3   49 R3

(Think of basic facts. 25 ÷ 5 = 5)

3,184 ÷ 8 ≈ 3,200 [÷] 8 = 400   3,184 [INT÷] 8 = $_Q$ 398 $_R$ 0   398

(Think of basic facts. 32 ÷ 8 = 4)

Problem	Estimate Quotient	Exact Quotient
1. 319 ÷ 4		
2. 444 ÷ 7		
3. 576 ÷ 8		
4. 6)414		
5. 9)777		
6. 3)1,175		
7. 5)1,935		
8. 6)1,789		

9. Why are your exact quotients less than or greater than your estimates?

_____

_____

Use with pages 172–173.

Name _____

Technology Master 18

Using a Calculator to Divide with 1-Digit Numbers

Suggested Technology: Calculator—Math Explorer or equivalent

You can use estimation and your calculator to improve your number sense when dividing by 1-digit numbers.

In each problem, three digits are given. Use estimation to determine which digit belongs in each blank. Then use the ÷ on your calculator to check the quotients.

Digits to use	Division Problem	Digits to use	Division Problem
1. 2, 2, 9	4)‾7̄3̄_	**2.** 4, 5, 6	6)‾7̄6̄_
3. 8, 4, 0	_)‾5̄5̄4	**4.** 1, 3, 7	_)‾5̄9̄7
5. 1, 4, 4	6)‾6̄9̄_	**6.** 2, 2, 5	9)‾5̄8̄_
7. 1, 2, 8	_)‾6̄4̄5	**8.** 3, 7, 7	_)‾9̄1̄6

9. What strategies did you use to place the digits in the blanks?

_____

_____

10. Did you need fewer tries for each guess as you did the problems? Why?

_____

18 Use with pages 182–183.

Name _____

Technology Master 19

Using a Calculator to Divide Money

Suggested Technology: Calculator—Math Explorer or equivalent

When you divide money you can use the [FIX] key to round your quotient to the nearest cent. Remember, use the [.] key to enter dollars and cents.

Example	Press	Display	Answer
6)$8.75	8.75 [÷] 6 [=] [FIX] 2	1.46	$1.46
	Use [FIX] 2 to get a decimal with 2 places after the decimal point.	Round to the nearest cent.	

You can also press [FIX] 2 and then enter the problem for the same result.

Use your calculator to find the quotients to the nearest cent. Try both methods.

Problem	Divide and round.	Use the [FIX] key.
1. 3)$4.66	_____	_____
2. 5)$10.44	_____	_____
3. 6)$45.20	_____	_____
4. 7)$59.56	_____	_____
5. 4)$92.46	_____	_____
6. 9)$427.20	_____	_____

Use with pages 196–199.

Using a Calculator to Divide Greater Numbers

Suggested Technology: Calculator—Math Explorer or equivalent

You can use the [INT÷] key to find the quotient and remainder when dividing.

Use the [INT÷] key to find the quotient and remainder and to complete the cross-number puzzle. Include "R" for remainder in the puzzle answers when necessary.

Example	**Press**	**Display**	**Answer**
472 ÷ 5	472 [INT÷] 5 [=]	94 2	94 R2

Across

1. 79 ÷ 5 _____
4. 1,707 ÷ 3 _____
5. 356 ÷ 4 _____
7. 2,671 ÷ 6 _____
8. 4,955 ÷ 8 _____

Down

1. 896 ÷ 7 _____
2. 590 ÷ 13 _____
3. 484 ÷ 7 _____
6. 18,862 ÷ 2 _____

Here's how to use the [÷] to find the quotient and remainder.

Example		**Press**	**Display**	**Answer**
472 ÷ 5	Step 1: Divide	472 [÷] 5 [=]	94.4	94 whole number part
	Step 2: Multiply	94 [×] 5 [=]	470	
	Step 3: Subtract	472 − 470 [=]	2	2 remainder

The quotient and remainder is 94 R2.

Find the quotient and remainder for each division problem using the [÷] key.

a. 412 ÷ 8 _____   b. 305 ÷ 2 _____   c. 288 ÷ 6 _____

d. 244 ÷ 9 _____   e. 377 ÷ 5 _____   f. 999 ÷ 8 _____

Name _____

Technology Master 21

Using a Computer to Find the Mean

Suggested Technology: Spreadsheet—ClarisWorks or equivalent

You can use a computer to find the mean of a set of numbers.

Example: What is the mean number of hours for the space missions listed in the table?

A. Enter the table into a spreadsheet.
- Choose **New** from the **FILE** menu.
- Select **Spreadsheet**, then click **OK**.
- Label the columns "U.S. Missions" and "Hours." Enter each space mission and its length in hours.

	A	B
1	U.S. Missions	Hours
2	Endeavor	260
3	Discovery	199
4	Columbia	354
5		

B. Find the mean number of hours.
- Type "Mean" in cell A5. Click on the cell to the right of "Mean."
- Choose **Paste Function** from the **EDIT** menu.
- Select **AVERAGE**, then click **OK**. In the entry bar, highlight all of the text in between the parentheses, type B2..B4. Press the **Return** key.

C. Graph your results.
- Highlight all of the cells in the table.
- Choose **Make Chart** from the **OPTIONS** menu. Click **Bar**.

Use the graph to answer the questions.

1. Which mission(s) was longer than the mean? Shorter?

   _____

2. Is a bar graph the best choice of graph for this data? Explain.

   _____

Explore

Find the number of students in 5 classes in your school. Use the computer to find the mean number of students per class.

_____

Use with pages 258–259.

Name _____

Technology Master 22

Using a Computer to Explore Quadrilaterals

Suggested Technology: Software—ClarisWorks or other drawing program

Open a new Draw Document.

A. Draw a rectangle.
- Look at the tool panel
- Click the rectangle tool.
- Drag the mouse to the drawing area and move it diagonally until you form a rectangle in the top part of the drawing area. Then release the mouse button.

1. Are a rectangle's sides of equal length?

_____

_____

B. Draw a square.
- Click the rectangle tool.
- Hold down the *Shift* key as you drag the mouse to draw a square in the middle of the drawing area.

2. Are a square's sides of equal length? Are a square's angles equal?

_____

C. Draw a parallelogram, rhombus, or trapezoid.
- Click the polygon tool. Drag the mouse to the bottom of the drawing area. Click to make the first side of the shape. Repeat to make more sides. To close the shape, move the mouse back to the starting point and click.

3. Are all the sides of this shape of equal length?

_____

D. Compare the shapes you drew. How are they alike? How are they different?

Explore

Use the painting tools in the tool panel to fill in your quadrilaterals with color, patterns, or shading.

22 Use with pages 276–277.

Name _____

Technology Master 23

Using a Calculator to Simplify Fractions

Suggested Technology: Calculator—Math Explorer or equivalent

You can use the [/], [SIMP], [x↔y], and [=] keys on your calculator to simplify fractions. You may have to press these keys several times to show a fraction in simplest form.

Example: Simplify $\frac{8}{12}$

Press: **Display:**

8 [/] 12   8/12

[SIMP] [=]   N/D → n/d 4/6

[x↔y]   2 ← The factor 2 was used by the calculator.

[x↔y] [SIMP] [=]   2/3

[x↔y]   2 ← The factor 2 was used by the calculator.

[x↔y]   2/3 ← N/D → n/d does not appear, so the fraction is in lowest terms.

The simplest form of $\frac{8}{12}$ is $\frac{2}{3}$.

Use the [/], [SIMP], [x↔y], and [=] keys on your calculator to simplify each fraction. Record each fraction you see in the display. Record the factor that the calculator uses each time to simplify the fraction.

1. $\frac{18}{24}$ _____ 2. $\frac{16}{40}$ _____ 3. $\frac{16}{100}$ _____

   factors: _____   factors: _____   factors: _____

4. $\frac{20}{50}$ _____ 5. $\frac{24}{36}$ _____ 6. $\frac{30}{75}$ _____

   factors: _____   factors: _____   factors: _____

7. How can you tell when you get the simplest fraction on your calculator?

_____

_____

Name _____

Technology Master 24

Using a Calculator to Compare and Order Fractions

Suggested Technology: Calculator—Math Explorer or equivalent

You can use the [F⇔D] key on your calculator to help you compare and order fractions. The [F⇔D] key changes a fraction to a decimal.

Example:	Press:	Display:
Compare $\frac{3}{8}$ and $\frac{1}{2}$	3 [/] 8 [F⇔D]	0.375
	1 [/] 2 [F⇔D]	0.5

Compare the decimals 0.375 and 0.5.
Since 0.375 is less than 0.5,   0.375 < 0.5
$\frac{3}{8}$ is less than $\frac{1}{2}$. $\frac{3}{8} < \frac{1}{2}$

Use the [F⇔D] key to help you compare each pair of fractions.

Write the decimal for each fraction. Then write <, =, or > in each ☐.

1. $\frac{1}{2}$ ☐ $\frac{3}{4}$ 2. $\frac{2}{3}$ ☐ $\frac{2}{5}$ 3. $\frac{5}{8}$ ☐ $\frac{5}{6}$

   ___ ☐ ___   ___ ☐ ___   ___ ☐ ___

4. $\frac{8}{12}$ ☐ $\frac{2}{3}$ 5. $\frac{7}{8}$ ☐ $\frac{2}{3}$ 6. $\frac{2}{3}$ ☐ $\frac{5}{6}$

   ___ ☐ ___   ___ ☐ ___   ___ ☐ ___

Write the decimal for each fraction. Round decimals to the nearest thousandth. Order the decimals and fractions from least to greatest.

Set of Fractions	Change Fractions to Decimals [F⇔D]	Order the Decimals	Order the Fractions
7. $\frac{1}{2}, \frac{1}{3}, \frac{1}{4}$	_____	_____	_____
8. $\frac{2}{3}, \frac{3}{4}, \frac{4}{7}, \frac{5}{8}$	_____	_____	_____

9. How can you change a fraction to a decimal if your calculator does not have a [F⇔D] key?

_____

Name _____

Technology Master 25

Using a Calculator to Convert Improper Fractions to Mixed Numbers

Suggested Technology: Calculator—Math Explorer or equivalent

You can use the [ab/c] key on your calculator to express an improper fraction as a mixed number. Then you can use the [SIMP] and [=] keys to simplify the mixed number. Remember: If the answer is a whole number, that's the simplest form. Pressing [SIMP] [=] will give an error code. Also, remember to press [SIMP] [=] several times. The first answer isn't always the simplest form.

Example:	Press:	Display:	
Express $\frac{10}{8}$ as a mixed number in simplest form.	10 [/] 8	10/8	
	[ab/c]	1u 2/8 ←	This is the mixed number $1\frac{2}{8}$. The "u" stands for "unit."
	[SIMP] [=]	1u 1/4	

The improper fraction $\frac{10}{8}$ expressed as the simplest mixed number is $1\frac{1}{4}$.

$$\frac{10}{8} = 1\frac{2}{8} = 1\frac{1}{4}$$

Use the [ab/c] and [SIMP] [=] keys to express these improper fractions as mixed numbers in simplest form.

1. $\frac{15}{6}$ _____ 2. $\frac{18}{9}$ _____ 3. $\frac{28}{10}$ _____ 4. $\frac{36}{8}$ _____

5. $\frac{21}{3}$ _____ 6. $\frac{25}{9}$ _____ 7. $\frac{18}{15}$ _____ 8. $\frac{42}{4}$ _____

9. $\frac{28}{7}$ _____ 10. $\frac{56}{8}$ _____ 11. $\frac{25}{4}$ _____ 12. $\frac{90}{60}$ _____

Do the following key sequences:

Fraction	Press	Display
$\frac{15}{6}$	15 [/] 6 [ab/c]	_____
$\frac{15}{6}$	15 [INT÷] 6 [=]	_____

13. How are the numbers in the displays the same?

_____

Use with pages 324–325. **25**

Name _____

Technology Master 26

Using a Calculator to Connect Fractions, Decimals, and Percents

Suggested Technology: Calculator—Math Explorer or equivalent

You can use your calculator to connect fractions, decimals, and percents.

	Example:	Press	Display
Fraction to a Decimal Use [F⇌D] key.	$\frac{5}{8}$	5 [/] 8 [F⇌D]	0.625
Decimal to a Fraction Use [F⇌D] key and [SIMP] keys.	0.75	0 [.] 75 [F⇌D] [SIMP] [=] [SIMP] [=]	75/100 15/20 3/4
Percent to a Decimal Use [%] key.	45%	45 [%]	0.45
Percent to a Fraction Use [%], [F⇌D] and [SIMP] keys.	45%	45 [%] [F⇌D] [SIMP] [=]	0.45 $\frac{45}{100}$ $\frac{9}{20}$

IMPORTANT: Save this page to use as a study guide.

Use your calculator to complete the chart. Express the fractions in simplest form.

	Fraction	Decimal	Percent
1.	$\frac{3}{5}$	_____	_____
2.	_____	0.25	_____
3.	$\frac{9}{10}$	_____	_____
4.	_____	_____	8%
5.	$2\frac{3}{4}$	_____	_____

6. How could you change a percent to a decimal without using a [%] key?

_____

_____

Use with pages 336–337.

Name _____

Technology Master 27

Using a Calculator to Find the Least Common Denominator

Suggested Technology: Calculator—Math Explorer or equivalent

To find the least common denominator (LCD) of two or more fractions, you can find the multiples of their denominators. Use the [Cons] key on your calculator to list multiples of a number.

Example

Find the LCD of $\frac{5}{6}$ and $\frac{3}{4}$.

Multiples of 6: **Press** [+] 6 [Cons][Cons][Cons][Cons] . . . The first multiple common
Display 6, 12, 18, 24, 30 . . . to both 6 and 4 is 12.

Multiples of 4: **Press** [+] 4 [Cons][Cons][Cons][Cons] . . . So, the LCD of $\frac{5}{6}$ and
Display 4, 8, 12, 16, 20, 24 . . . $\frac{3}{4}$ is 12.

Use the [Cons] key on your calculator to list the multiples of each denominator for each set of fractions. Then write the LCD.

1. $\frac{4}{9}$ and $\frac{5}{6}$

    9: _____
    6: _____
    LCD: _____

2. $\frac{1}{8}$ and $\frac{7}{10}$

    8: _____
    10: _____
    LCD: _____

3. $\frac{7}{9}$ and $\frac{3}{8}$

    9: _____
    8: _____
    LCD: _____

4. $\frac{11}{12}$ and $\frac{1}{30}$

    12: _____
    30: _____
    LCD: _____

5. $\frac{3}{4}$, $\frac{1}{8}$, and $\frac{5}{12}$

    4: _____
    8: _____
    12: _____
    LCD: _____

6. Write a pair of fractions. Find the multiples of each denominator. Then write the LCD.

    _____
    _____

Use with pages 352–353.

Name _____

Technology Master 28

Using a Calculator to Add Fractions and Mixed Numbers

Suggested Technology: Calculator—Math Explorer or equivalent

You can use your calculator to find the length of a path on the figure at the right.

- Use the [/] and [Unit] keys to show fractions and mixed numbers on your calculator.
- Use the [ab/c] and [SIMP] keys to help you express the answer in simplest form.

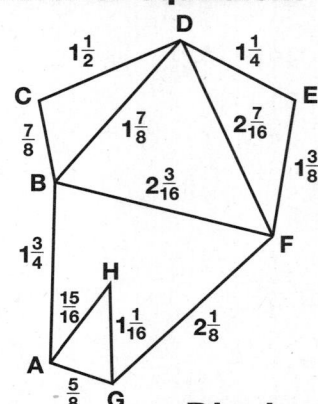

Example	Press	Display
Path *BCD*	7 [/] 8 [+] 1 [Unit] 1 [/] 2 [=] [ab/c]	1u 11/8 2u 3/8
Path *EFG*	1 [Unit] 3 [/] 8 [+] 2 [Unit] 1 [/] 8 [=] [SIMP] [=] [SIMP] [=]	3u 4/8 3u 2/4 3u 1/2

Find the length of each path. Write the fractions and mixed numbers for each path. Use your calculator to add and to express the answer in simplest form.

1. Path *CDE*

_____ + _____ = _____

2. Path *ABC*

_____ + _____ = _____

3. Path *HAB*

_____ + _____ = _____

4. Path *CBF*

_____ + _____ = _____

5. Perimeter of triangle *DEF*

_____ + _____ + _____ = _____

6. Perimeter of quadrilateral *ABFG*

_____ + _____ + _____ + _____ = _____

28 Use with pages 384–385.

Name _____

Technology Master 29

Using a Calculator to Explore Feet, Yards, and Miles

Suggested Technology: Calculator—Math Explorer or equivalent

	Examples	Press	Display
• To change smaller units to larger units, divide. Use the [INT÷] key.	Change 45 inches to yards.	45 [INT÷] 36 [=] (1 yd = 36 in.) So, 45 in. = 1 yd 9 in.	1 Q 9 R
• To change larger units to smaller units, multiply. Use the [×] key.	Change 8 yards to feet.	8 [×] 3 [=] (1 yd = 3 ft.) So, 8 yd = 24 ft	24

Use the [INT÷] or [×] keys on your calculator to complete the table.

| 1 ft = 12 in. | 1 yd = 3 ft | 1 mi = 1,760 yd |
| | 1 yd = 36 in. | 1 mi = 5,280 ft |

Length	Change to	Write multiply or divide.	Copy the display.	Write answer with units.
1. 5 ft	in.	_____	_____	_____
2. 5 ft	yd	_____	_____	_____
3. 43 ft	yd	_____	_____	_____
4. 2 mi	yd	_____	_____	_____
5. 10,000 ft	mi	_____	_____	_____
6. 3 mi	yd	_____	_____	_____
7. 2,000 yd	mi	_____	_____	_____
8. 444 in.	ft	_____	_____	_____

Circle which measure is more. Then tell why.

9. 5 ft 8 in. or 58 in.

10. 50 yd or 100 ft

11. 11 yd 2 ft or 36 ft

12. 1 mi or 1795 yd

Use with pages 390–391.

Name _____

Technology Master 30

Using a Calculator to Find the Products of Fractions, Mixed Numbers, and Whole Numbers

Suggested Technology: Calculator—Math Explorer or equivalent

You can use the ⟦/⟧, ⟦×⟧, ⟦UNIT⟧ and ⟦=⟧ keys to multiply a fraction or mixed number by a whole number on your calculator. Use rounding to estimate the product first. Use the ⟦ab/c⟧ and/or the ⟦SIMP⟧ key to simplify your answers.

Examples	Estimate	Press	Display
$\frac{4}{7} \times 19$	Round $\frac{4}{7}$ to $\frac{1}{2}$; $\frac{1}{2} \times 20 = 10$	4 ⟦/⟧ 7 ⟦×⟧ 19 ⟦=⟧ ⟦ab/c⟧	76/7 10u6/7

The estimate 10 is close to $10\frac{6}{7}$.

$1\frac{7}{8} \times 6$	Round $1\frac{7}{8}$ to 2; $2 \times 6 = 12$	1 ⟦UNIT⟧ 7 ⟦/⟧ 8 ⟦×⟧ 6 ⟦=⟧ ⟦ab/c⟧ ⟦SIMP⟧⟦=⟧	90/8 11u2/8 11u1/4

The estimate 12 is close to $11\frac{1}{4}$.

Estimate each product. Then use your calculator to find the exact product in simplest form.

1. $\frac{4}{5} \times 18$ _____ _____

2. $1\frac{5}{8} \times 9$ _____ _____

3. $\frac{5}{6} \times 25$ _____ _____

4. $\frac{4}{9} \times 28$ _____ _____

5. $1\frac{3}{8} \times 33$ _____ _____

6. $\frac{5}{6} \times 43$ _____ _____

7. $\frac{3}{11} \times 16$ _____ _____

8. $3\frac{7}{8} \times 6$ _____ _____

Use with pages 407–408.

Name _____

Technology Master 31

Using a Calculator to Multiply Whole Numbers by Fractions

Suggested Technology: Calculator—Math Explorer or equivalent

Use the ⌹, ⌧, and ⌸ keys to multiply whole numbers by fractions. You can use the F⇄D key to change the product to a decimal.

The circle graph shows the production of about 290 million metric tons of wheat in four top-producing countries of the world.

How many metric tons of wheat were produced in the United States?

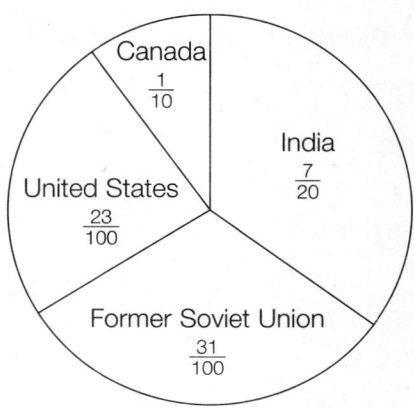

World Wheat Production Among Top 4 Countries

Press	**Display**
23 ⌹ 100 ⌧ 290 ⌸	6670/100
ab/c	66u70/100
F⇄D	66.7

The United States produced about 66.7 million tons of wheat.

Use your calculator to solve each problem. Write each answer in decimal form.

1. How many metric tons of wheat were produced in India? _____

2. How many metric tons of wheat were produced in the former Soviet Union? _____

3. How many metric tons of wheat were produced in Canada? _____

4. How many more tons of wheat were produced in India than in the United States? _____

5. How many tons of wheat were produced in the United States and Canada? _____

Use with pages 420–421. **31**

Name _____

Technology Master 32

Using a Calculator to Multiply Whole Numbers and Mixed Numbers

Suggested Technology: Calculator—Math Explorer or equivalent

Use the ☒, [UNIT], [/], and [=] keys to multiply whole and mixed numbers.
Use the [ab/c] key to convert improper fractions to whole or mixed numbers.

This is Frank's favorite brownie recipe.

Frank's Fudge Brownies

$2\frac{1}{2}$ cups sugar
$1\frac{2}{3}$ cups margarine
5 (1-oz) squares chocolate
4 large eggs
$1\frac{3}{4}$ cups all-purpose flour
$1\frac{1}{3}$ cups chopped nuts
$\frac{1}{2}$ cup milk
$1\frac{1}{4}$ tsp vanilla extract

How many cups of sugar would Frank need if he increased the recipe 6 times?

Press	Display
6 ☒ 2 [UNIT] 1 [/] 2 [=]	30/2
[ab/c]	15

Frank would need 15 cups of sugar.

Use your calculator and the recipe above to solve the following problems.

How many cups of margarine would Frank need if he increased the recipe 5 times? _____

How many cups of all-purpose flour would Frank need if he increased the recipe 8 times? _____

How many teaspoons of vanilla extract would Frank need if he increased the recipe 5 times? _____

How many cups of chopped nuts would Frank need if he increased the recipe 3 times? _____

How many squares of chocolate would Frank need if he increased the recipe $2\frac{1}{2}$ times? _____

If this recipe makes 4 dozen brownies, what would you need to multiply the amount of each ingedient by to make 6 dozen brownies? _____

Use with pages 422–423.

Name _____

Technology Master 33

Using a Calculator to Find the Perimeters of Polygons

Suggested Technology: Calculator—Math Explorer or equivalent

The distance around a polygon is its **perimeter.**

You can use the ⊕ and ⊜ keys to find the perimeter of *any polygon* by adding the lengths of its sides.

Example: Find the perimeter of the following triangle:

(triangle with sides 4 cm, 5 cm, 6 cm)

Press: **Display:**

4 ⊕ 5 ⊕ 6 ⊜   15

The perimeter is 15 cm.

You can use the ⊗ and ⊜ keys to find the perimeter of a regular polygon by multiplying the length of one side by the number of sides.

Example: Find the perimeter of the equilateral triangle:

(equilateral triangle with side 4 cm)

Press: **Display:**

3 ⊗ 4 ⊜   12

The perimeter is 12 cm.

Use your calculator to find the perimeter of each polygon. Write the perimeter with units. (All polygons with only 1 side labeled are regular.)

1. _____
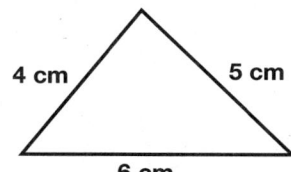

2. _____

3. _____
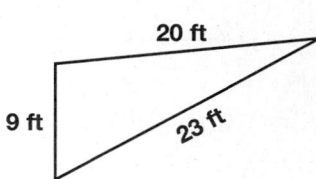

4. _____
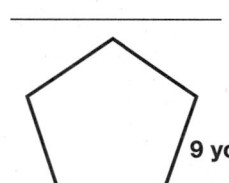

5. _____
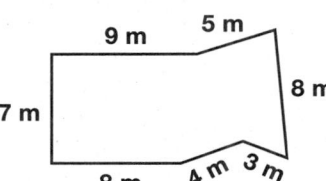

6. _____
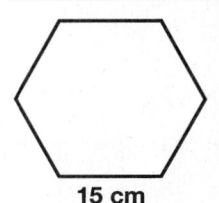

7. What is the perimeter of a square whose sides measure 18 meters each? _____

Use with pages 450–451.   **33**

Name _____

Technology Master 34

Using a Calculator to Find the Perimeters of Rectangles

Suggested Technology: Calculator—Math Explorer or equivalent

You can use your calculator to find the perimeter of a rectangle by applying either of the following formulas:

$P = 2(l + w)$. $P = 2l + 2w$.

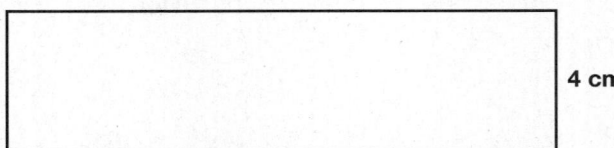

For $P = 2(15 + 4)$, use the ⊠, ⊡, ⊕, ⊡, and ⊟ keys:

Press: **Display:**
2 ⊠ ⊡ 15 ⊕ 4 ⊡ ⊟   38

The perimeter is 38 cm.

For $P = 2 \times 15 + 2 \times 4$, use the ⊠, ⊕, and ⊟ keys:

Press: **Display:**
2 ⊠ 15 ⊕ 2 ⊠ 4 ⊟   38

The perimeter is 38 cm.

Use your calculator to find the perimeter of each rectangle. Use either formula.

1. _____   2. _____   3. _____

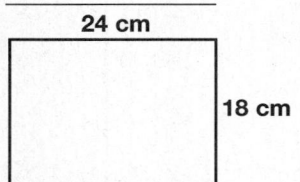 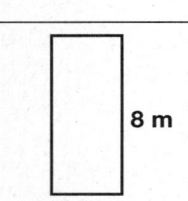 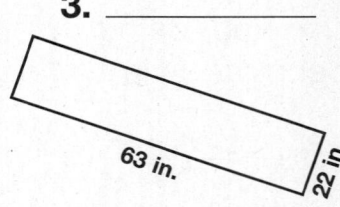

Use your calculator to find the missing length or width of each rectangle. Hint: you will need to use the ⊕ and ⊖ keys.

4. $P = 80$ ft, $w =$ _____

5. $P = 288$ yd, $w =$ _____

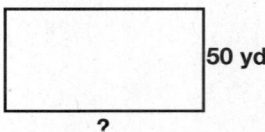

6. Find three whole-number solutions for the length and width of a rectangle with $P = 12$ cm.

_____

_____

34 Use with pages 452–453.

Name _____

Technology Master 35

Using a Calculator to Convert Units to Find Perimeter

Suggested Technology: Calculator—Math Explorer or equivalent

You can use your calculator to find the perimeter of a polygon whose sides are given in two kinds of units:

- Convert to like units.
- Add the sides of the polygon.
- Express the answer in simplest form.

Remember:
1 ft = 12 in. or 1 in. = $\frac{1}{12}$ ft
1 yd = 3 ft or 1 ft = $\frac{1}{3}$ yard

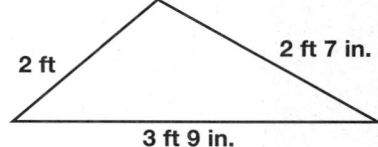

Example: Find the perimeter of the triangle first in inches, then in feet.

To find the perimeter in inches:

Press:	Display:
Side 1: 2 [×] 12 [=]	24
Side 2: [+] [(] 2 [×] 12 [+] 7 [)]	31
Side 3: [+] [(] 3 [×] 12 [+] 9 [)]	45
Total: [=]	100

Change 100 inches back to feet/inches:
100 [INT÷] 12 [=]   Q⎣8⎦ R⎣4⎦

8 is the quotient (Q) and 4 is the remainder (R).
So, the perimeter is 100 inches or 8 feet 4 inches.

To find the perimeter in feet:

Press:	Display:
2	2
[+] 2 [Unit] 7 [/] 12	2u 7/12
[+] 3 [Unit] 9 [/] 12	3u 9/12
[=]	7u 16/12
[ab/c]	8u 4/12
[SIMP] [=] [SIMP] [=]	8u 1/3

The perimeter is $8\frac{1}{3}$ feet.

Use your calculator to find the perimeter both ways.

1. P = _____ ft _____ in.
   or P = _____ ft

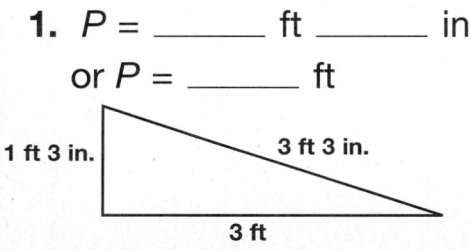

2. P = _____ yd _____ ft
   or P = _____ ft

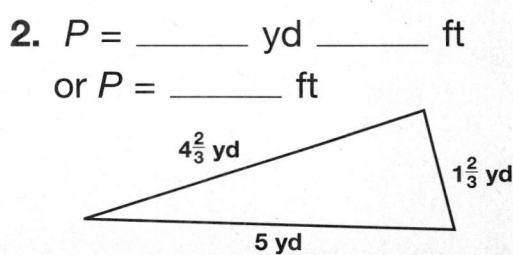

Use with pages 454–455. **35**

Name _____

Technology Master 36

Using a Calculator to Find the Area of Rectangles

Suggested Technology: Calculator—Math Explorer or equivalent

The **area** is measured in *square units*.

You can use your calculator to apply this formula to find the area of a rectangle:

Area = length × width
$A = l \times w$

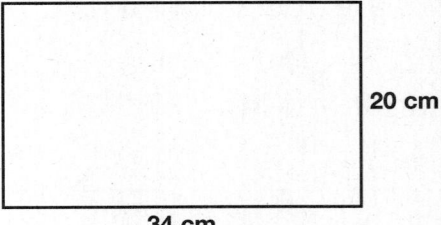

Press: **Display:**

34 ⊠ 20 ▭   *680*   The area is 680 cm².

↑   ↑
length   width

Use your calculator to find the area of each rectangle. Write the area in square units. (Figure 6 is a square.)

1. _____ 2. _____ 3. _____

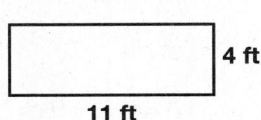 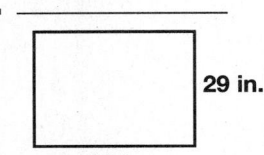 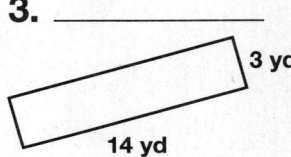

4. _____ 5. _____ 6. _____

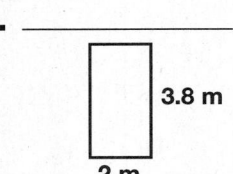 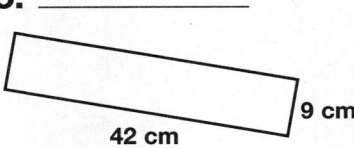 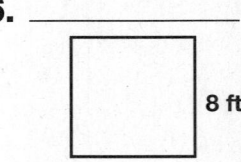

Use your calculator to find the missing length or width of each rectangle. (Hint: Use your ÷ key.)

7. $A = 80$ in², $w =$ _____

8. $A = 150$ cm², $l =$ _____

9. Find five whole-number solutions for the lengths and widths of rectangles, each with an area of 36 ft². Draw pictures of the rectangles on grid paper.

_____

Name _____

Technology Master 37

Using a Calculator to Find Area of Triangles

Suggested Technology: Calculator—Math Explorer or equivalent

You can use your calculator to apply this formula to find the area of a triangle:

Count the units of the height.
Count the units of the base.

Area = $\frac{1}{2}$ (base × height)

$A = \frac{1}{2}(b \times h)$ or $A = \frac{1}{2} \times b \times h$

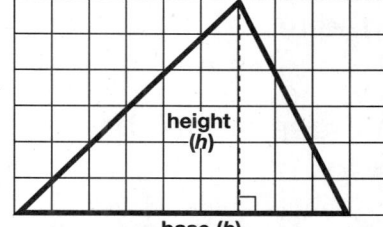

Example: Find the area of the triangle in square units.

Press: **Display:**

1 [/] 2 [×] 9 [×] 6 [=] [SIMP] [=]   27/1   The area is 27 units^2.
       ↑   ↑
    base height

Use your calculator to find the area of each triangle. Write the area in square units.

1. _____
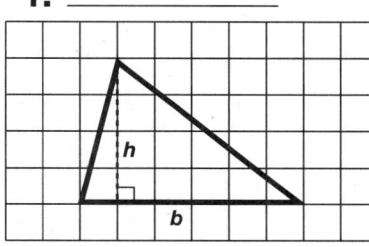

2. _____
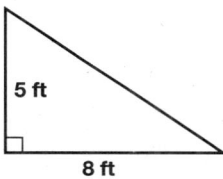

3. _____
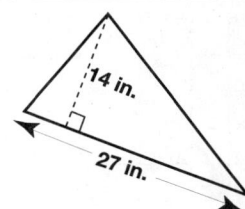

4. Use your calculator to find the area of each face and of the base of this square pyramid. Then find the total area. (Hint: A square pyramid has 4 faces and a base.)

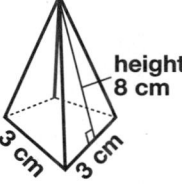

_____

_____

© Scott Foresman Addison Wesley 5

Use with pages 466–467. **37**

Name _____

Technology Master 38

Using a Calculator to Find the Area of Parallelograms

Suggested Technology: Calculator—Math Explorer or equivalent

You can use your calculator to apply this formula to find the area of a parallelogram:

Count the units of the height.
Count the units of the base.

Area = base × height
$A = b \times h$

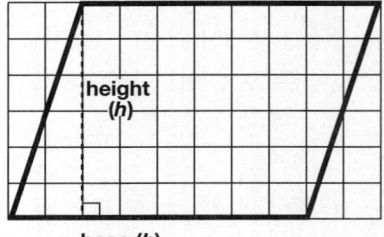

Example: Find the area in square units:

Press: **Display:**

8 ⊠ 6 ⊟   48   The area is 48 units².
↑   ↑
base height

Use your calculator to find the area of each parallelogram. Write the area in square units.

1. _____   2. _____   3. _____

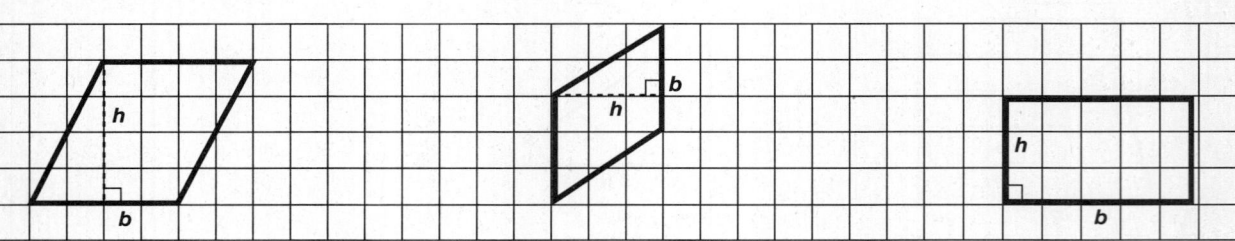

4. _____   5. _____   6. _____

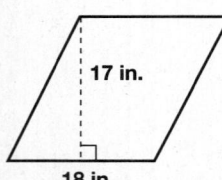 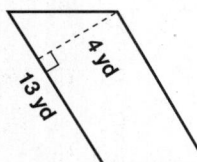 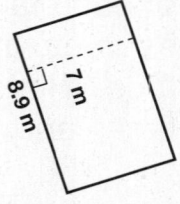

Use your calculator to find the area and perimeter of each parallelogram.

7. 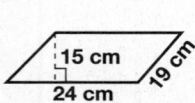   A = _____   8. A = _____
   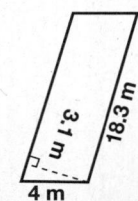
   P = _____   P = _____

38   Use with pages 470–471.

Name _____

Technology Master 39

Using a Calculator to Explore Circumference

Suggested Technology: Calculator—Math Explorer or equivalent

The distance around a circle is its **circumference.** The circumference is about 3 times longer than the diameter and is measured in *units.* You can use a calculator to apply this formula to find the circumference of a circle.

Circumference = π × diameter or π × 2 × radius
$C = \pi d$ $\pi = 3.14$ $C = \pi \times 2r$

The calculator uses a more precise decimal for π. Press the [π] key to see it! Use the [FIX] key to fix π to a certain number of decimal places.

Example: Find the circumference of a circle with a diameter of 8 cm. Solve the problem 3 ways to see how the answers differ.

Use the [π] key:		Round [π] to hundredths:		Use [π] ≈ 3.14:	
Press:	**Display:**	**Press:**	**Display:**	**Press:**	**Display:**
[π]	3.1415927	[FIX] 2 [π]	3.14	3 [.] 14	3.14
[×] 8 [=]	25.132741	[×] 8 [=]	25.13	[×] 8 [=]	25.12

↑ diameter

The circumference is about 25 cm.

Use your calculator to find the circumference 3 ways.

Diameter or Radius	Use [π] key	Use [FIX] 2 [π] keys	Use 3.14
1. d = 10 m			
2. r = 6 in.			
3. d = 15 ft			
4. r = 9 yd			
5. d = 22 cm			
6. r = 13 m			

Use with pages 476–477.

Name _____

Technology Master 40

Using a Calculator to Find Surface Area

Suggested Technology: Calculator—Math Explorer or equivalent

The **surface area** of any solid is equal to the sum of the areas of all of its faces. Surface area is measured in *square units*.

This is the formula for the surface area of any rectangular prism:

Surface area = (2 × front area)
+ (2 × side area)
+ (2 × top area)
= total area of faces

You can use the memory keys [M+] and [MR] on your calculator to find surface area. The [M+] key adds a number to the memory. The [MR] key displays the contents of the memory.

Press	Display
2 × 5 × 6 = M+	60
2 × 3 × 6 = M+	36
2 × 3 × 5 = M+	30
MR	126

The surface area is 126 m².

Use your calculator to find the surface area of each rectangular prism.

1.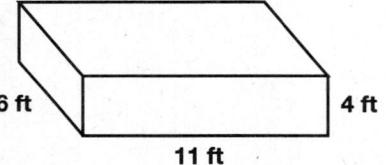

   Surface area = _____

2.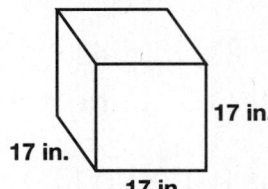

   Surface area = _____

3.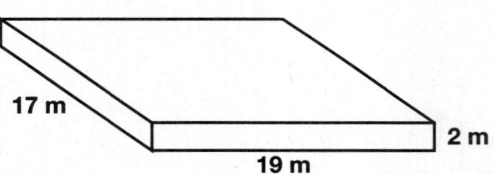

   Surface area = _____

4.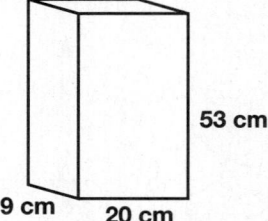

   Surface area = _____

5. Find the width of this solid if the surface area is 268 m². _____

   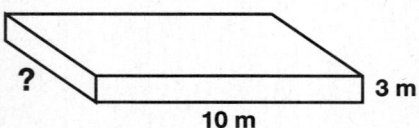

6. Show how to find the surface area of one of the solids above using the parentheses keys (and) instead of the memory keys.

   _____

   _____

   _____

40 Use with pages 494–495.

Name _____

Technology Master 41

Using a Calculator to Explore Ounces, Pounds, and Tons

Suggested Technology: Calculator—Math Explorer or equivalent

- When changing larger units to smaller units, *multiply*. Use the [×] and [=] keys.

Example	Press	Display	
5 T = ___ lb	5 [×] 2000 [=]	10000	5 T = 10,000 lb

Remember: 1 T = 2,000 lb

- When changing smaller units to larger units, divide. Use the [INT÷] and [=] keys. The number above the Q is the quotient. The number above the R is the remainder.

Example	Press	Display	
43 oz = ___ lb	43 [INT÷] 16 [=]	2 Q 11 R	43 oz = 2 lb 11 oz

Remember: 1 lb = 16 oz

Use your calculator and the measurement facts above to complete the problems.

Circle [×] ___ or [INT÷] ___, then fill in the blank. Problem 1 has been done for you.

1. 9 lb [×] 16 = 144 oz
   [INT÷] ___

2. 14,000 lb [×] ___ = ___ T
   [INT÷] ___

3. 18 T [×] ___ = ___ lb
   [INT÷] ___

4. 125 oz [×] ___ = ___ lb ___ oz
   [INT÷] ___

5. 1,000 oz [×] ___ = ___ lb ___ oz
   [INT÷] ___

6. 54,321 lb [×] ___ = ___ T ___ lb
   [INT÷] ___

7. Find 1 T = _____ oz. How did you get your answer?

_____

Use your calculator to convert each pair of measurements to the same unit. Then write <, >, or = in each ◯.

8. 6 lb ◯ 72 oz

   ___ ◯ 72 oz

9. 5 T ◯ 15,000 lb

   ___ ◯ 15,000 lb

Use with pages 500–501. **41**

Name _____

Technology Master 42

Using a Calculator to Find Volume

Suggested Technology: Calculator—Math Explorer or equivalent

The **volume** of a solid is the number of *cubic units* it contains. You can find the volume of a rectangular prism by using a formula and your calculator.

Example Volume = length × width × height   **Press**   **Display**

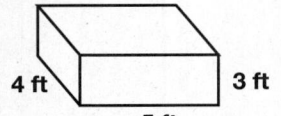

$V = l \times w \times h$
$V = 5 \text{ ft} \times 4 \text{ ft} \times 3 \text{ ft}$

5 [×] 4 [×] 3 [=]   60

The volume is 60 ft³. ← cubic units

Use your calculator to find the volume of each rectangular prism.

1.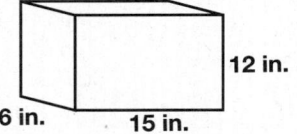

V = _____

2.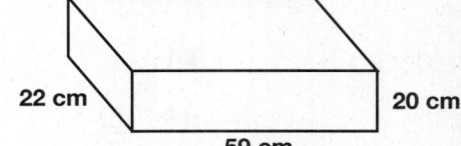

V = _____

3.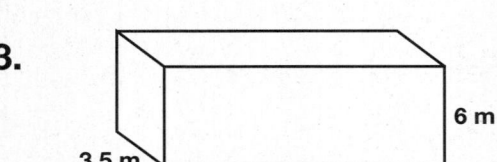

V = _____

4.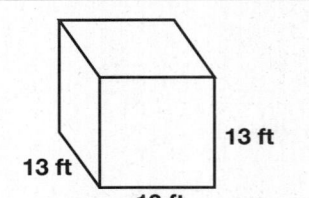

V = _____

Now find the volume of these solids.

5.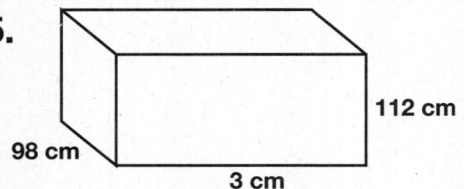

V = _____

6.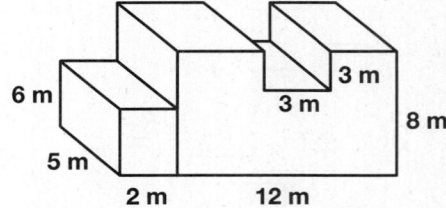

V = _____

Find the surface area of the solids in Problems 1–4 above.

1. _____

2. _____

3. _____

4. _____

42   Use with pages 508–509.

Name _____

Technology Master 43

Using a Calculator to Find Measurements for a Scale Drawing

Suggested Technology: Calculator—Math Explorer or equivalent

Use the scale drawing and your calculator to determine the actual measurements of the rooms in this house. Each square on the grid paper is 20 inches by 20 inches. Give each room's length and width in inches and then in feet and inches.

Example: Living Room

Press	Display
Length (units)	
7 × 20 =	140
Width (units)	
11 × 20 =	220

140 inches by 220 inches

Press	Display
140 INT÷ 12 =	11 R 8
220 INT÷ 12 =	18 R 4

11 ft 8 in. by 18 ft 4 in.

Scale: 20 in.

Room	Inches	Feet and Inches
Living Room	140 in. by 220 in.	11 ft 8 in. by 18 ft 4 in.
Dining Room		
Bedroom		
Bathroom		
Kitchen		
Hall		
Outside Walls		

Use with pages 536–537.

Name _____

Technology Master 44

Using a Calculator to Find the Percent of a Number

Suggested Technology: Calculator—Math Explorer or equivalent

Discount Warehouse

10-speed Bike $159.00 Sale 15% off	Space Watches $49.95 Any style 20% off	CD Players $89.00 Special 25% off
Comedy Videos $18.00 Discounted 33%	Headphones $34.75 Save 20%	CD Caddy $37.50 Super Sale—10% off

You can use your calculator to find the discount and sale price.

Example	Press	Display	Amount

What is the discount and sale price of a space watch?

Discount → 49.95 [×] 20 [%] [=]   9.99 $9.99

Sale Price → 49.95 [−] 9.99 [=]   39.96 $39.96
                 ↑   ↑
        Original price Discount

Discount is $9.99. Sale price is $39.96.

1. How much do you save when you buy the CD player on sale?

   _____

2. What is the amount of discount on the 10-speed bike?

   _____

3. What is the sale price of the CD Caddy?

   _____

4. How much money do you pay for a set of headphones on sale?

   _____

5. How much will it cost to buy 4 comedy videos on sale?

   _____

6. What is the total cost of a 10-speed bike on sale with 6% sales tax added to it?

   _____

Technology Master 1

Using a Calculator to Solve Problems: Choose the Operation

Suggested Technology: Calculator—Math Explorer or equivalent

This bar graph shows how much money 4 high school students earned during the summer for 1 month. How much more money did Kayla earn than Cody?

The graph shows that Kayla earned $90 and Cody earned $30.

Press [ON/C]

Press 9 0 [−] 3 0 [=]

Display shows: 6 0.

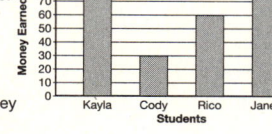

Since this problem involves money amounts, the answer is $60.

Kayla earned $60 more than Cody.

Use your calculator and the bar graph above to solve each problem. First read the problem and choose the operation. Show the keys to press and what the display will show. Then label each answer.

	Press	Display	Answer
1. How much money did Rico and Cody earn in 1 month?	60 + 30 =	90	$90
2. How much money will Cody earn at this rate in 3 months?	30 × 3 =	90	$90
3. If Janell is paid $5 an hour, how many hours did she work?	80 ÷ 5 =	16	16 hours

4. Make up your own problem using the information from the bar graph. Have a classmate use a calculator to solve the problem.

Answers will vary.

Use with pages 20–21. 1

Technology Master 2

Using a Calculator to Explore Algebra

Suggested Technology: Calculator—Math Explorer or equivalent

You can use the [Cons] key to complete T tables by following these steps:

Step 1: Press the rule and the [Cons] key.
Step 2: Press each number in Column A followed by the [Cons].
Step 3: Write each display in Column B.

Example Rule: $n \times 3$ Press [×] 3 [Cons]

A	B		Press		Display
2	6		2 [Cons]		6.
5	15		5 [Cons]		15.
6	18		6 [Cons]		18.

[CE/C] to clear

Use the [Cons] key to complete each T table. Write the keys you will press for the first two tables.

1. Rule: $n \times 8$ Press [×] 8 [Cons]   **2.** Rule: $n \div 7$ Press [÷] 7 [Cons]

A	B	Press	Display		A	B	Press	Display
12	96	12 [Cons]	96		91	13	91 [Cons]	13
32	256	32 [Cons]	256		84	12	84 [Cons]	12
61	488	61 [Cons]	488		63	9	63 [Cons]	9
13	104	13 [Cons]	104		133	19	133 [Cons]	19

3. Rule: $n + 12$ **4.** Rule: $n - 29$ **5.** Rule: $n - 4$

A	B		A	B		A	B
23	35		94	65		10	6
37	49		81	52		15	11
76	88		41	12		20	16
44	56		68	39		25	21

2 Use with pages 22–23.

Technology Master 3

Using a Calculator to Solve Line Graph Problems

Suggested Technology: Calculator—Math Explorer or equivalent

This line graph shows the number of cars sold by one car dealership in a 12-month period. How many cars were sold in all from January through March?

The graph shows that in January 50 cars were sold, in February 60 were sold, and in March 55 were sold.

Press [ON/C] then

Press 5 0 [+] 6 0 [+] 5 5 [=]

Display shows: 165. 165 cars were sold in all from January through March.

Use your calculator and the line graph above to solve each problem. Show the keys to press, the display, and your answer.

	Press	Display	Answer
1. How many more cars were sold in September than in April?	110 − 95 =	15	15 more cars
2. How many more cars were sold in September than in December and January combined?	110 − 50 − 50 =	10	10 more
3. If the same number of cars were sold each of 4 weeks in February, how many cars were sold each week?	60 ÷ 4 =	15	15 per week

4. Make up a problem based on the line graph above. Have a classmate use a calculator to solve it.

Answers will vary.

Use with pages 32–33. 3

Technology Master 4

Using a Computer to Make a Graph

Suggested Technology: Spreadsheet—ClarisWorks or equivalent

A group of fifth graders found the following information about the daily and Sunday circulation of 5 newspapers:

The Dallas News: Daily–504 thousand; Sunday–834 thousand
Miami Herald: Daily–414 thousand; Sunday–543 thousand
Star-Tribune: Daily–414 thousand; Sunday–696 thousand
Inquirer: Daily–503 thousand; Sunday–965

A. Create a table for the data.
- Choose **New** from the **FILE** menu.
- Select **Spreadsheet**, then click **OK**.
- Click on the rows and columns of the table as you complete the information as shown below:

	Newspapers	Daily	Sunday
1	Dallas	504	834
2	Miami	414	543
3	Star	414	696
4	Inquirer	503	965

B. Make a graph of the data.
- Highlight all of the cells in the table.
- Choose **Make Chart** from the **OPTIONS** menu.
- Look at all the graphs. Click on your choice of graph.
- Click on **Labels**, then enter a new title for your graph. Click **OK**.

Use the table and the graph to answer these questions.
1. Which newspaper has the greatest circulation? **Inquirer**
2. Which newspaper has the lowest? **Miami**
3. Are daily or Sunday circulations higher in general? **Sunday**

4 Use with pages 40–41.

45

Name _____   **Technology Master 5**

Using the Calculator to Explore Place Value through Millions

Suggested Technology: Calculator—Math Explorer or equivalent

You can use your calculator to add or subtract numbers written in word form.

Example:

Four hundred fifty-two thousand, one hundred thirty-five **plus** five hundred forty-seven thousand, eight hundred sixty-five.

Press: `4 5 2 1 3 5 +` `5 4 7 8 6 5 =`   Display: `1000000`

The answer with commas is 1,000,000.

Complete the following using your calculator. Put commas in the Displays.

	Press:	Display:
1. Two million, eight hundred thousand **minus** one million, seven hundred thousand.	2,800,000 `−` 1,700,000 `=`	1,100,000
2. Eight hundred forty-six thousand, thirty-eight **plus** fifty-three thousand, nine hundred sixty-two.	846,038 `+` 53,962 `=`	900,000
3. Six million four hundred thousand, five hundred **minus** five million five hundred ninety-nine thousand, seven hundred.	6,400,500 `−` 5,599,700 `=`	800,800
4. Seven hundred eighty-nine thousand, three hundred **plus** two hundred one thousand, six hundred nine.	789,300 `+` 201,609 `=`	990,909
5. One million, one hundred one thousand, one **minus** two hundred twenty thousand, nine hundred ninety-three.	1,101,001 `−` 220,993 `=`	880,008

6. How did you decide where to place your commas? **Counted every three digits from the right.**

Use with pages 54–55. **5**

Name _____   **Technology Master 6**

Using a Calculator to Explore Place-Value Relationships

Suggested Technology: Calculator—Math Explorer or equivalent

You can use a calculator to find the values for greater factors of 10. Use the `×` and `=` keys to complete the pattern.

Factors of 10	Press	Display	Number name
10	1`×`10`=`	10	ten
10×10	1`×`10`=``=`	100	one hundred
10×10×10	1×10===	1000	one thousand
10×10×10×10	1×10====	10000	thousand
10×10×10×10×10	1×10=====	100000	one hundred thousand
10×10×10×10×10×10	1×10======	1000000	one million

What pattern do you see? **As each factor increases by one, the number of zeros does too.**

How many factors of 10 can you use your calculator to find the value for? Why? **7, after that an Error 0 shows**

You can use a calculator to find the value of 10 in exponent forms. Use the `10ⁿ` key and the number of the exponent to complete the pattern.

Exponent form	Press	Display	Number name
10^1	`10ⁿ` 1	10	ten
10^2	`10ⁿ` 2	100	one hundred
10^3	`10ⁿ` 3	1000	one thousand
10^4	`10ⁿ` 4	10000	ten thousand
10^5	`10ⁿ` 5	100000	one hundred thousand
10^6	`10ⁿ` 6	1000000	one million

What pattern do you see? **the same number of zeros as the exponent**

What is the greatest power of 10 you can evaluate using your calculator? Why **10^7, after that an Error 0 shows**

6 Use with pages 56–57.

Name _____   **Technology Master 7**

Using a Computer to Compare and Order Numbers

Suggested Technology: Spreadsheet—ClarisWorks or equivalent

You can use your computer to compare the population of some states in 1950 with their population in 1990.

A. Create a table for your data. Choose **New** from the **FILE** menu. Select **Spreadsheet**, then click **OK**.

1. Click on the rows and columns of the table as you fill in the information as shown below:

	A	B	C
1	States	1950	1990
2	Alaska	129,000	550,000
3	Delaware	318,000	666,000
4	North Dakota	620,000	639,000
5	South Dakota	653,000	696,000
6	Vermont	378,000	563,000
7	Wyoming	291,000	454,000

B. Highlight all of the cells in the table. Choose **Make Chart** from the **OPTIONS** menu. Look at the different graphs available. Choose the one you think best shows the data. Click on **Labels**, then enter a new title for the graph. Click **OK**.

2. Which graph did you choose? Explain. **Answers will vary.**

3. Which state's population doubled from 1950 to 1990? **Delaware**

4. Which state's population was about four times more in 1990 than in 1950? **Alaska**

5. Which states had more people in 1950 than either Alaska, Vermont, or Wyoming had in 1990? **North Dakota and South Dakota**

6. Write the states in order from least to greatest population in 1950. **Alaska, Wyoming, Delaware, Vermont, North Dakota, South Dakota**

Use with pages 60–61. **7**

Name _____   **Technology Master 8**

Using the Calculator to Explore Thousandths

Suggested Technology: Calculator—Math Explorer or equivalent

You can use your calculator to play "Wipe Out."

- Enter a decimal number that has tenths, hundredths, and thousandths. Make each digit different. Do not use zero.
- Use addition or subtraction to change the "Wipe Out" number to zero.

Example: The number is 26.413. The "Wipe Out" number is 3.

Use subtraction.	Or use addition.
Press `2 6 . 4 1 3`	Press `2 6 . 4 1 3`
Display 26.413	Display 26.413
Press `− 0 . 0 0 3 =`	Press `+ 0 . 0 0 7 =`
Display 26.41	Display 26.41

Now try these.

	Decimal Number	"Wipe Out" Number"	Your Method
1.	23.976	9	Subtract 0.9 or Add 0.1
2.	456.789	5	Subtract 50 or Add 50
3.	3.842	4	Subtract 0.04 or Add 0.06
4.	12.953	3	Subtract 0.003 or Add 0.007
5.	2.385	2	Subtract 2 or Add 8
6.	382.671	1	Subtract 0.001 or Add 0.009

7. What conclusion can you make about the two numbers that can wipe out a digit? **Their digits add up to 10.**

8. Make up your own "Wipe Out" example. Choose a decimal number. Choose a digit to wipe out. Have a friend solve it. **Answers will vary.**

8 Use with pages 70–71.

Name _____

Technology Master 9

Using a Calculator to Round Decimals

Suggested Technology: Calculator—Math Explorer or equivalent

You can use the [FIX] key to round decimals. Press [FIX] 1 to round to the nearest tenth (1 decimal place), or [FIX] 2 to round to the nearest hundredth (2 decimal places) and then enter the number to be rounded.

Example 1: Round 0.378 to the nearest tenth.

Press [FIX][1][.][3][7][8]   Display 0.4

Press [FIX] 2 to round to the nearest hundredth (2 decimal places).

Example 2: Round 0.378 to the nearest hundredth.

Press [FIX][2][.][3][7][8]   Display 0.38

Use the [FIX] key to complete the following table.

	Decimal Number	Rounded to the nearest tenth	Rounded to the nearest hundredth
1.	0.6753	0.7	0.68
2.	2.563	2.6	2.56
3.	3.0865	3.1	3.09
4.	12.782	12.8	12.78
5.	0.00876	0.0	0.01
6.	0.123	0.1	0.12
7.	5.5555	5.6	5.56

Explore

8. How do you think you could use your calculator to round a decimal to the nearest thousandth? [FIX] 3

9. Use your method to round 1.8769 to the nearest thousandth.
1.877

10. Did your method work? How can you tell?
Yes, because when you follow rules for rounding, 1.8769 rounds to the nearest thousandth is 1.877.

Use with pages 76–77. 9

Name _____

Technology Master 10

Using the Calculator to Add Whole Numbers

Suggested Technology: Calculator—Math Explorer or equivalent

Use the distances on the U.S. map and your calculator to find the total distance traveled. The first one is done for you.

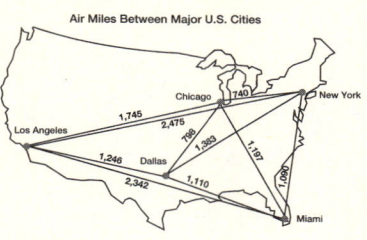

Air Miles Between Major U.S. Cities

Total Distance

1. Los Angeles to Chicago to New York City
   Press [1][7][4][5][+][7][4][0][=]   2,485 mi

2. New York City to Miami to Los Angeles to Chicago
   Press [1][0][9][0][+][2][3][4][2][+][1][7][4][5][=]   **5,177 mi**

3. Round trip between Los Angeles and New York City
   Press [2][4][7][5][+][2][4][7][5][=]   **4,950 mi**

4. Round trip between Dallas and Chicago.
   Press [7][9][8][+][7][9][8][=]   **1,596 mi**

5. Suppose you could earn a free trip by traveling a total of 25,000 miles. What trips would you take to earn the free trip (if you live in Miami)?

Possible answer: 5 round-trips to Los Angeles (23,420 mi) and 1 round-trip to Dallas (2,220 mi); 25,640 mi

10 Use with pages 84–87.

Name _____

Technology Master 11

Using the Calculator to Add and Subtract Decimals

Suggested Technology: Calculator—Math Explorer or equivalent

Use your calculator to find the missing numbers in these magic squares. In a magic square, the sum is the same for the numbers in each row, column, and diagonal.

Here's how to find the first missing number:

Press [7][.][7][4][−][3][.][3][9][−][2][.][8][5][=]   Display 1.5

Use this strategy to find the rest.

Magic Sum: 7.74

3.39	1.5	2.85
2.04	2.58	3.12
2.31	3.66	1.77

Magic Sum: 5.6

2.6	0.7	1.2	1.1
0.5	1.8	1.3	2
0.8	1.5	1	2.3
1.7	1.6	2.1	0.2

Magic Sum: 3.9

0.66	1.08	1.5	0.12	0.54
0.6	0.72	1.14	1.26	0.18
0.24	0.36	0.78	1.2	1.32
1.38	0.3	0.42	0.84	0.96
1.02	1.44	0.06	0.48	0.9

What strategy did you use to find the missing numbers?

Found rows and columns with only 1 missing number. Subtracted all the other numbers from the magic sum. That display was always the missing number.

Use with pagess 94–97. 11

Name _____

Technology Master 12

Using the Calculator to Explore Place Value Relationships

Suggested Technology: Calculator—Math Explorer or equivalent

Use the [×] and [=] keys to find the largest possible product for each set of digits. The first is done for you.

1. Make the greatest product. Use digits 2, 7, 9.

   7 2
   ×   9
   ———
   648

   Press   Display
   27 × 9 =   243
   92 × 7 =   644
   72 × 9 =   648

2. Make the least product. Use digits 2, 7, 9.

   7 9
   ×   2
   ———
   158

3. Make the greatest product of a 1-digit and a 3-digit number. Use digits 1, 3, 4, 8.

   4 3 1
   ×   **8**
   ———
   3,448

4. Make the least product of a 1-digit and a 3-digit number. Use digits 1, 3, 4, 8.

   3 4 8
   ×   **1**
   ———
   348

5. Make the greatest product of two 2-digit numbers. Use digits 1, 3, 4, 8.

   8 1
   × **4 3**
   ———
   3,483

6. Make the least product of two 2-digit numbers. Use digits 1, 3, 4, 8.

   3 8
   × **1 4**
   ———
   532

7. Make the greatest product of a 2-digit and a 3-digit number. Use digits 5, 6, 7, 8, 9.

   8 7 5
   ×   **9 6**
   ———
   84,000

8. Make the least product of a 2-digit and a 3-digit number. Use digits 5, 6, 7, 8, 9.

   5 7 9
   ×   **6 8**
   ———
   39,372

12 Use with pages 116–119.

Name _____

Technology Master 13

Using a Calculator to Find Multiples of Numbers

Suggested Technology: Calculator—Math Explorer or equivalent

You can use the [=] key on your calculator to find the least common multiple (LCM) of two or more numbers.

Examples:

Numbers	Press [=] at least 5 times	Display	LCM
8	+8 [=][=][=][=][=]	8, 16, 24, 32, ㊵	
10	+10 [=][=][=][=][=]	10, 20, 30, ㊵, 50	40

40 is the least common multiple of 8 and 10.

Note: If there is no common multiple to either number after pressing the [=] key 5 times, press the [=] key several more times for each number.

Use a calculator to find the LCM for each set of numbers.

	Numbers	Press [=]	Display	LCM
1.	6	+6 [=][=][=][=][=]	6, 12, 18, ㉔, 30	
	8	+8 [=][=][=][=][=]	8, 16, ㉔, 32, 40	24
2.	8	+8 [=][=][=][=][=]	8, 16, ㉔, 32, 40	
	12	+12 [=][=][=][=][=]	12, ㉔, 36, 48, 60	24
3.	5	+5 [=][=][=][=][=] [=][=][=]	5, 10, 15, 20, 25, 30, 35, 40, ㊺	
	9	+9 [=][=][=][=][=]	9, 18, 27, 36, ㊺	
	15	+15 [=][=][=][=][=]	15, 30, ㊺, 60, 75	45
4.	4	+4 [=][=][=][=][=]	4, 8, 12, 16, ⑳	
	5	+5 [=][=][=][=][=]	5, 10, 15, ⑳, 25	
	10	+10 [=][=][=][=]	10, ⑳, 30, 40, 50	20

Use with pages 126–127. 13

Name _____

Technology Master 14

Using a Calculator to Perform Order of Operations

Suggested Technology: Calculator—Math Explorer or equivalent

You can use two different methods on a calculator to solve problems using the order of operations.

Example: Solve using the order of operations: $(7 + 8) - (12 \div 4)$.

Method 1: Use [(] and [)] keys.

Press	Display
[(] 7 [+] 8 [)] [-] [(] 12 [÷] 4 [)] [=]	12

When you use these keys just input the numbers and ( ) in the order they are in. The calculator does the math in the correct order.

Method 2: Use [M+], [M-], and [MR] keys.

Press	Display
7 [+] 8 [=] [M+] 12 [÷] 4 [=] [M-] [MR]	12

The [M+] key saves 7 + 8 in memory. The [M-] key subtracts 12 ÷ 4 from the first amount. The [MR] key shows the results.

Use both methods on your calculator to solve each problem. Write the keys you press for each method and the display.

	Method 1: [(] [)] Press	Display	Method 2: [M+], [M-], [MR] Press	Display
1. $(14 \times 6) - (5 \times 6)$	[(]14[×]6[)][-] [(]5[×]6[)][=]	54	14[×]6[=][M+] 5[×]6[=][M-][MR]	54
2. $52 - (12 \div 3 \times 2)$	52[-][(]12[÷] 3[×]2[)][=]	44	52[M+] 12[÷] 3[×]2[=][M-][MR]	44
3. $(18 - 3) + (6 \times 5 \div 2)$	[(]18[-]3[)][+] [(]6[×]5[÷]2[)][=]	30	18[-]3[=][M+] 6[×]5[÷]2[=][M+][MR]	30
4. $75 + (32 \div 4 + 6)$	75[+][(]32[÷] 4[+]6[)][=]	89	75[M+] 32[÷] 4[+]6[=][M+][MR]	89
5. $(76 - 32 \div 4) - 60$	[(]76[-]32 [÷]4[)][-]60[=]	8	76[-]32[÷]4[=] [M+]60[M-][MR]	8

6. Which method did you prefer? Why? **Answers will vary.**

14 Use with pages 130–131.

Name _____

Technology Master 15

Using a Calculator to Solve Multiple-Step Problems

Suggested Technology: Calculator—Math Explorer or equivalent

You can use the [(] and [)] keys or the [M+] and [MR] keys to solve multiple-step problems.

Delicious Deli Delights					
Potato Salad $1.25/lb	Turkey Bologna $1.99/lb	Honey Roast Ham $3.99/lb	Smoked Turkey $4.35/lb	Lovely Liverwurst $3.59/lb	Provolone Cheese $3.79/lb

Example: How much would you pay for:

	Press using [M+] and [MR] keys.	Display	Solution
3 lb potato salad	3 [×] 1.25 [=] [M+]	3.75	
1 lb cheese	3.79 [M+]	3.79	
2 lb ham	2 [×] 3.99 [=] [M+] [MR]	7.98 15.52	$15.52
Using parentheses.	[(]3 [×] 1.25[)] [+] 3.79 [+] [(]2 [×] 3.99[)] [=]	15.52	$15.52

Find the cost.

	Press using [M+] and [MR] keys.	Display	Solution
1. 3 lb smoked turkey	3 [×] 4.35 [=] [M+]	13.05	
1 lb liverwurst	3.59 [M+]	3.59	
2 lb cheese	2 [×] 3.79 [=] [M+] [MR]	7.58	$24.22
Using parentheses.	[(]3 [×] 4.35[)] [+] 3.59 [+] [(]2 [×] 3.79[)] [=]	24.22	$24.22
2. 5 lb bologna	5 [×] 1.99 [=] [M+]	9.95	
2 lb potato salad	2 [×] 1.25 [=] [M+] [MR]	2.5	$12.45
Using parentheses.	[(]5 [×] 1.99[)] [+] [(]2 [×] 1.25[)] [=]	12.45	$12.45

Use with pages 140–141. 15

Name _____

Technology Master 16

Using the Calculator to Multiply Decimals

Suggested Technology: Calculator—Math Explorer or equivalent

It is useful to estimate a product when you use a calculator just in case you press a wrong key or forget a number.

Make an estimate for each problem. Then find the decimal product. Use the [.] key.

Hint: Look at the whole number parts of the problem.

	Problem	Estimate	Product	Close	Not close
1.	Example: 4×3.92	$4 \times 4 = 16$	Press: 4 [×] 3.92 [=] Display: 15.68	✓	
2.	2.1×79	$2 \times 80 = 160$	165.9		
3.	3.9×1.2	$4 \times 1 = 4$	4.68		
4.	5.09×88	$5 \times 90 = 450$	447.92		
5.	82.0×9.0	$80 \times 9 = 720$	738		
6.	64×0.9	$60 \times 1 = 60$	57.6		
7.	0.4×0.79	$0.4 \times 0.8 = 0.32$	0.316		
8.	40×0.19	$40 \times 0.2 = 8$	7.6		
9.	320×0.49	$320 \times 0.5 = 160$	156.8		
10.	6.832×9.075	$7 \times 9 = 63$	62.0004		

How close were your estimates to the actual product? Mark "Close" or "Not close" in the chart.

Answers will vary.

16 Use with pages 146–149.

Name _____

Technology Master 17

Using a Calculator to Estimate Quotients and Remainders

Suggested Technology: Calculator—Math Explorer or equivalent

Use **compatible numbers** to estimate a quotient. Then use the [INT÷] key to find the exact quotient.

Examples: Estimate quotient. | Use [INT÷] key to find quotient. | Exact Quotient
Press | Display | Press | Display |

$248 \div 5 \approx$ 250 [÷] 5 = 50   248 [INT÷] 5 = _49_ R _3_   49 R3
(Think of basic facts. $25 \div 5 = 5$)

$3{,}184 \div 8 \approx$ 3,200 [÷] 8 = 400   3,184 [INT÷] 8 = _398_ R _0_   398
(Think of basic facts. $32 \div 8 = 4$)

Problem	Estimate Quotient	Exact Quotient
1. $319 \div 4$	$320 \div 4 = 80$	79 R3
2. $444 \div 7$	$420 \div 7 = 60$	63 R3
3. $576 \div 8$	$560 \div 8 = 70$	72
4. $6\overline{)414}$	$420 \div 6 = 70$	69
5. $9\overline{)777}$	$810 \div 9 = 90$	86 R3
6. $3\overline{)1{,}175}$	$1{,}200 \div 3 = 400$	391 R2
7. $5\overline{)1{,}935}$	$2{,}000 \div 5 = 400$	387
8. $6\overline{)1{,}789}$	$1{,}800 \div 6 = 300$	298 R1

9. Why are your exact quotients less than or greater than your estimates?
The dividend in the estimate was either rounded down or up to use compatible numbers to estimate the quotient.

Use with pages 172–173. **17**

Name _____

Technology Master 18

Using a Calculator to Divide with 1-Digit Numbers

Suggested Technology: Calculator—Math Explorer or equivalent

You can use estimation and your calculator to improve your number sense when dividing by 1-digit numbers.

In each problem, three digits are given. Use estimation to determine which digit belongs in each blank. Then use the [÷] on your calculator to check the quotients.

Digits to use	Division Problem	Digits to use	Division Problem
1. 2, 2, 9	$4\overline{)292}^{\,73}$	2. 4, 5, 6	$6\overline{)456}^{\,76}$
3. 8, 4, 0	$8\overline{)440}^{\,55}$	4. 1, 3, 7	$3\overline{)177}^{\,59}$
5. 1, 4, 4	$6\overline{)414}^{\,69}$	6. 2, 2, 5	$9\overline{)522}^{\,58}$
7. 1, 2, 8	$8\overline{)512}^{\,64}$	8. 3, 7, 7	$7\overline{)637}^{\,91}$

9. What strategies did you use to place the digits in the blanks?
Possible answer: I looked at the first digit in each quotient and then thought of basic facts for compatible numbers.

10. Did you need fewer tries for each guess as you did the problems? Why?
Answers will vary.

18 Use with pages 182–183.

Name _____

Technology Master 19

Using a Calculator to Divide Money

Suggested Technology: Calculator—Math Explorer or equivalent

When you divide money you can use the [FIX] key to round your quotient to the nearest cent. Remember, use the [.] key to enter dollars and cents.

Example | Press | Display | Answer
$6\overline{)\$8.75}$ | 8.75 [÷] 6 [FIX] 2 | 1.46 | $1.46
 | Use [FIX] 2 to get a decimal with 2 places after the decimal point. | Round to the nearest cent. |

You can also press [FIX] 2 and then enter the problem for the same result.

Use your calculator to find the quotients to the nearest cent. Try both methods.

Problem	Divide and round.	Use the [FIX] key.
1. $3\overline{)\$4.66}$	1.553333 $1.55	$1.55
2. $5\overline{)\$10.44}$	2.088 $2.09	$2.09
3. $6\overline{)\$45.20}$	7.533333 $7.53	$7.53
4. $7\overline{)\$59.56}$	8.5085714 $8.51	$8.51
5. $4\overline{)\$92.46}$	23.115 $23.12	$23.12
6. $9\overline{)\$427.20}$	47.466667 $47.47	$47.47

Use with pages 196–199. **19**

Name _____

Technology Master 20

Using a Calculator to Divide Greater Numbers

Suggested Technology: Calculator—Math Explorer or equivalent

You can use the [INT÷] key to find the quotient and remainder when dividing.

Use the [INT÷] key to find the quotient and remainder and to complete the cross-number puzzle. Include "R" for remainder in the puzzle answers when necessary.

Example | Press | Display | Answer
$472 \div 5$ | 472 [INT÷] 5 [=] | 94 R 2 | 94 R2

Across
1. $79 \div 5$ **15 R4**
4. $1{,}707 \div 3$ **569 R0**
5. $356 \div 4$ **89 R0**
7. $2{,}671 \div 6$ **445 R1**
8. $4{,}955 \div 8$ **619 R3**

Down
1. $896 \div 7$ **128 R0**
2. $590 \div 13$ **45 R5**
3. $484 \div 7$ **69 R1**
6. $18{,}862 \div 2$ **9,431 R0**

Cross-number puzzle:
1. **1 5 R 4** 2. **6**
2. **5 6 9**
5. **8** 6. **9** R R
7. **4 4 5 R 1**
3. **8 6 1 9 R 3**

Here's how to use the [÷] to find the quotient and remainder.
Example | Press | Display | Answer
$472 \div 5$ | Step 1: Divide 472 [÷] 5 [=] | 94.4 | 94 whole number part
 | Step 2: Multiply 94 [×] 5 [=] | 470 |
 | Step 3: Subtract 472 − 470 [=] | 2 | 2 remainder
The quotient and remainder is 94 R2.

Find the quotient and remainder for each division problem using the [÷] key.
a. $412 \div 8$ **51 R4** b. $305 \div 2$ **152 R1** c. $288 \div 6$ **48 R0**
d. $244 \div 9$ **27 R1** e. $377 \div 5$ **75 R2** f. $999 \div 8$ **124 R7**

20 Use with pages 234–237.

49

Name _____ **Technology Master 21**

Using a Computer to Find the Mean

Suggested Technology: Spreadsheet—ClarisWorks or equivalent

You can use a computer to find the mean of a set of numbers.

Example: What is the mean number of hours for the space missions listed in the table?

A. Enter the table into a spreadsheet.
  • Choose **New** from the **FILE** menu.
  • Select **Spreadsheet**, then click **OK**.
  • Label the columns "U.S. Missions" and "Hours." Enter each space mission and its length in hours.

	A	B
1	U.S. Missions	Hours
2	Endeavor	260
3	Discovery	199
4	Columbia	354
5	**Mean**	**271**

B. Find the mean number of hours.
  • Type "Mean" in cell A5. Click on the cell to the right of "Mean."
  • Choose **Paste Function** from the **EDIT** menu.
  • Select **AVERAGE**, then click **OK**. In the entry bar, highlight all of the text in between the parentheses, type B2..B4. Press the **Return** key.

C. Graph your results.
  • Highlight all of the cells in the table.
  • Choose **Make Chart** from the **OPTIONS** menu. Click **Bar**.

Use the graph to answer the questions.

1. Which mission(s) was longer than the mean? Shorter?
   Columbia; Discovery and Endeavor

2. Is a bar graph the best choice of graph for this data? Explain.
   Answers will vary.

Explore

Find the number of students in 5 classes in your school. Use the computer to find the mean number of students per class.
Answers will vary.

Use with pages 258–259. **21**

Name _____ **Technology Master 22**

Using a Computer to Explore Quadrilaterals

Suggested Technology: Software—ClarisWorks or other drawing program

Open a new Draw Document.

A. Draw a rectangle.
  • Look at the tool panel.
  • Click the rectangle tool ▢.
  • Drag the mouse to the drawing area and move it diagonally until you form a rectangle in the top part of the drawing area. Then release the mouse button.

1. Are a rectangle's sides of equal length?
   A side is of equal length to its opposite side, but the pairs of opposite sides may be of the same or different lengths.

B. Draw a square.
  • Click the rectangle tool.
  • Hold down the *Shift* key as you drag the mouse to draw a square in the middle of the drawing area.

2. Are a square's sides of equal length? Are a square's angles equal?
   Yes; yes

C. Draw a parallelogram, rhombus, or trapezoid.
  • Click the polygon tool. Drag the mouse to the bottom of the drawing area. Click to make the first side of the shape. Repeat to make more sides. To close the shape, move the mouse back to the starting point and click.

3. Are all the sides of this shape of equal length?
   No; Answers will vary as to exactly how the sides differ.

D. Compare the shapes you drew. How are they alike? How are they different?
   Answers will vary.

Explore

Use the painting tools in the tool panel to fill in your quadrilaterals with color, patterns, or shading.

22 Use with pages 276–277.

Name _____ **Technology Master 23**

Using a Calculator to Simplify Fractions

Suggested Technology: Calculator—Math Explorer or equivalent

You can use the ⌐/⌐, SIMP, ⌐→, and ⌐= keys on your calculator to simplify fractions. You may have to press these keys several times to show a fraction in simplest form.

Example: Simplify $\frac{8}{12}$

Press:	Display:
8 / 12	8/12
SIMP	N/D → n/d 4/6
⌐→	2 ← The factor 2 was used by the calculator.
⌐→ SIMP ⌐=	2/3
⌐→	2 ← The factor 2 was used by the calculator.
⌐→	2/3 ← N/D → n/d does not appear, so the fraction is in lowest terms.

The simplest form of $\frac{8}{12}$ is $\frac{2}{3}$.

Use the ⌐/⌐, SIMP, ⌐→, and ⌐= keys on your calculator to simplify each fraction. Record each fraction you see in the display. Record the factor that the calculator uses each time to simplify the fraction.

1. $\frac{18}{24}$ **9/12, 3/4** factors: **2, 3**
2. $\frac{16}{40}$ **8/20, 4/10, 2/5** factors: **2, 2, 2**
3. $\frac{16}{100}$ **8/50, 4/25** factors: **2, 2**
4. $\frac{20}{50}$ **10/25, 2/5** factors: **2, 5**
5. $\frac{24}{36}$ **12/18, 6/9, 2/3** factors: **2, 2, 3**
6. $\frac{30}{75}$ **10/25, 2/5** factors: **3, 5**

7. How can you tell when you get the simplest fraction on your calculator?
   When the N/D → n/d no longer appears, the fraction is in lowest terms.

Use with pages 312–313. **23**

Name _____ **Technology Master 24**

Using a Calculator to Compare and Order Fractions

Suggested Technology: Calculator—Math Explorer or equivalent

You can use the F↔D key on your calculator to help you compare and order fractions. The F↔D key changes a fraction to a decimal.

Example: Compare $\frac{3}{8}$ and $\frac{1}{2}$

Press:	Display:
3 / 8 F↔D	0.375
1 / 2 F↔D	0.5

Compare the decimals 0.375 and 0.5.
Since 0.375 is less than 0.5, $0.375 < 0.5$
$\frac{3}{8}$ is less than $\frac{1}{2}$. $\frac{3}{8} < \frac{1}{2}$

Use the F↔D key to help you compare each pair of fractions.
Write the decimal for each fraction. Then write <, =, or > in each ☐.

1. $\frac{1}{2}$ **<** $\frac{3}{4}$ 2. $\frac{2}{3}$ **>** $\frac{2}{5}$ 3. $\frac{5}{8}$ **<** $\frac{5}{6}$
   0.5 < 0.75   **0.667 > 0.4**   **0.625 < 0.833**

4. $\frac{8}{12}$ **=** $\frac{2}{3}$ 5. $\frac{7}{8}$ **>** $\frac{2}{3}$ 6. $\frac{2}{3}$ **<** $\frac{5}{6}$
   0.667 = 0.667   **0.875 > 0.667**   **0.667 < 0.833**

Write the decimal for each fraction. Round decimals to the nearest thousandth. Order the decimals and fractions from least to greatest.

Set of Fractions	Change Fractions to Decimals F↔D	Order the Decimals	Order the Fractions
7. $\frac{1}{2}, \frac{1}{3}, \frac{1}{4}$	**0.5, 0.333, 0.25**	**0.25, 0.333, 0.5**	**$\frac{1}{4}, \frac{1}{3}, \frac{1}{2}$**
8. $\frac{2}{3}, \frac{3}{4}, \frac{4}{7}, \frac{5}{8}$	**0.667, 0.75, 0.571, 0.625**	**0.571, 0.625, 0.667, 0.75**	**$\frac{4}{7}, \frac{5}{8}, \frac{2}{3}, \frac{3}{4}$**

9. How can you change a fraction to a decimal if your calculator does not have a F↔D key?
   Use the ÷ key to divide the numerator by the denominator.

24 Use with pages 314–315.

Technology Master 25

Using a Calculator to Convert Improper Fractions to Mixed Numbers

Suggested Technology: Calculator—Math Explorer or equivalent

You can use the [A♭⁄c] key on your calculator to express an improper fraction as a mixed number. Then you can use the [SIMP] and [=] keys to simplify the mixed number. Remember: If the answer is a whole number, that's the simplest form. Pressing [SIMP] [=] will give an error code. Also, remember to press [SIMP] [=] several times. The first answer isn't always the simplest form.

Example:

	Press:	Display:
Express $\frac{10}{8}$	10 [/] 8	10/8
as a mixed number in simplest form.	[A♭⁄c]	1u 2/8 ← This is the mixed number $1\frac{2}{8}$. The "u" stands for "unit."
	[SIMP] [=]	1u 1/4

The improper fraction $\frac{10}{8}$ expressed as the simplest mixed number is $1\frac{1}{4}$.

$\frac{10}{8} = 1\frac{2}{8} = 1\frac{1}{4}$

Use the [A♭⁄c] and [SIMP] [=] keys to express these improper fractions as mixed numbers in simplest form.

1. $\frac{15}{6}$ = **$2\frac{1}{2}$**
2. $\frac{18}{9}$ = **2**
3. $\frac{28}{10}$ = **$2\frac{4}{5}$**
4. $\frac{36}{8}$ = **$4\frac{1}{2}$**
5. $\frac{21}{3}$ = **7**
6. $\frac{25}{9}$ = **$2\frac{7}{9}$**
7. $\frac{18}{15}$ = **$1\frac{1}{5}$**
8. $\frac{42}{4}$ = **$10\frac{1}{2}$**
9. $\frac{28}{7}$ = **4**
10. $\frac{56}{8}$ = **7**
11. $\frac{25}{4}$ = **$6\frac{1}{4}$**
12. $\frac{90}{60}$ = **$1\frac{1}{2}$**

Do the following key sequences:

Fraction	Press	Display
$\frac{15}{6}$	15 [/] 6 [A♭⁄c]	**$2u\frac{3}{6}$**
$\frac{15}{6}$	15 [INT÷] 6 [=]	**2 3** (Q R)

13. How are the numbers in the displays the same?
They both show 2 whole units with a remainder of 3.

Use with pages 324–325.

Technology Master 26

Using a Calculator to Connect Fractions, Decimals, and Percents

Suggested Technology: Calculator—Math Explorer or equivalent

You can use your calculator to connect fractions, decimals, and percents.

	Example:	Press	Display
Fraction to a Decimal Use [F↔D] key.	$\frac{5}{8}$	5 [/] 8 [F↔D]	0.625
Decimal to a Fraction Use [F↔D] key and [SIMP] keys.	0.75	0 [.] 75 [F↔D]	75/100
		[SIMP] [=]	15/20
		[SIMP] [=]	3/4
Percent to a Decimal Use [%] key.	45%	45 [%]	0.45
Percent to a Fraction Use [%], [F↔D] and [SIMP] keys.	45%	45 [%]	0.45
		[F↔D]	$\frac{45}{100}$
		[SIMP] [=]	$\frac{9}{20}$

IMPORTANT: Save this page to use as a study guide.

Use your calculator to complete the chart. Express the fractions in simplest form.

Fraction	Decimal	Percent
1. $\frac{3}{5}$	**0.6**	**60%**
2. **$\frac{1}{4}$**	0.25	**25%**
3. $\frac{9}{10}$	**0.9**	**90%**
4. $\frac{2}{25}$	**0.08**	8%
5. $2\frac{3}{4}$	**2.75**	**275%**

6. How could you change a percent to a decimal without using a [%] key?
Possible answer: For 25%, think of $\frac{25}{100}$ and press 25 [÷] 100 [=] to get 0.25.

Use with pages 336–337.

Technology Master 27

Using a Calculator to Find the Least Common Denominator

Suggested Technology: Calculator—Math Explorer or equivalent

To find the least common denominator (LCD) of two or more fractions, you can find the multiples of their denominators. Use the [Cons] key on your calculator to list multiples of a number.

Example

Find the LCD of $\frac{5}{6}$ and $\frac{3}{4}$.

Multiples of 6: Press [×] 6 [Cons] [Cons] [Cons] . . .
Display 6, 12, 18, 24, 30 . . .   The first multiple common to both 6 and 4 is 12.

Multiples of 4: Press [×] 4 [Cons] [Cons] [Cons] . . .
Display 4, 8, 12, 16, 20, 24 . . .   So, the LCD of $\frac{5}{6}$ and $\frac{3}{4}$ is 12.

Use the [Cons] key on your calculator to list the multiples of each denominator for each set of fractions. Then write the LCD.

1. $\frac{4}{9}$ and $\frac{5}{6}$
   9: **9, 18, 27, 36 ...**
   6: **6, 12, 18, 24, 30 ...**
   LCD: **18**

2. $\frac{1}{8}$ and $\frac{7}{10}$
   8: **8, 16, 24, 32, 40, 48 ...**
   10: **10, 20, 30, 40 ...**
   LCD: **40**

3. $\frac{7}{9}$ and $\frac{3}{8}$
   9: **9, 18, 27, 36, 45, 54, 63, 72, 81 ...**
   8: **8, 16, 24, 32, 40, 48, 56, 64, 72 ...**
   LCD: **72**

4. $\frac{11}{12}$ and $\frac{1}{30}$
   12: **12, 24, 36, 48, 60, 72, 84 ...**
   30: **30, 60 ...**
   LCD: **60**

5. $\frac{3}{4}$, $\frac{1}{8}$, and $\frac{5}{12}$
   4: **4, 8, 12, 16, 20, 24, 28 ...**
   8: **8, 16, 24, 32, 40 ...**
   12: **12, 24, 36, 48 ...**
   LCD: **24**

6. Write a pair of fractions. Find the multiples of each denominator. Then write the LCD.

Use with pages 352–353.

Technology Master 28

Using a Calculator to Add Fractions and Mixed Numbers

Suggested Technology: Calculator—Math Explorer or equivalent

You can use your calculator to find the length of a path on the figure at the right.

- Use the [/] and [A♭⁄c] keys to show fractions and mixed numbers on your calculator.
- Use the [A♭⁄c] and [SIMP] keys to help you express the answer in simplest form.

Example	Press	Display
Path BCD	7 [/] 8 [+] 1 1 [/] 2 [=] [A♭⁄c]	1u 11/8 2u 3/8
Path EFG	1 3 [/] 8 [+] 2 1 [/] 8 [=]	3u 4/8
	[SIMP] [=]	3u 2/4
	[SIMP] [=]	3u 1/2

Find the length of each path. Write the fractions and mixed numbers for each path. Use your calculator to add and to express the answer in simplest form.

1. Path CDE
   $1\frac{1}{2} + 1\frac{1}{4} = 2\frac{3}{4}$

2. Path ABC
   $1\frac{3}{4} + \frac{7}{8} = 1\frac{13}{8} = 2\frac{5}{8}$

3. Path HAB
   $\frac{15}{16} + 1\frac{3}{4} = 1\frac{27}{16} = 2\frac{11}{16}$

4. Path CBF
   $\frac{7}{8} + 2\frac{3}{16} = 2\frac{17}{16} = 3\frac{1}{16}$

5. Perimeter of triangle DEF
   $1\frac{1}{4} + 1\frac{3}{8} + 2\frac{7}{16} = 4\frac{17}{16} = 5\frac{1}{16}$

6. Perimeter of quadrilateral ABFG
   $1\frac{3}{4} + 2\frac{3}{16} + 2\frac{1}{8} + \frac{5}{8} = 5\frac{27}{16} = 6\frac{11}{16}$

Use with pages 384–385.

Technology Master 29
Using a Calculator to Explore Feet, Yards, and Miles

Suggested Technology: Calculator—Math Explorer or equivalent

- To change smaller units to larger units, divide. Use the [INT÷] key.
  - Change 45 inches to yards.
  - Examples: 45 [INT÷] 36 [=]
  - Display: 1 r 9
  - (1 yd = 36 in.)
  - So, 45 in. = 1 yd 9 in.

- To change larger units to smaller units, multiply. Use the [×] key.
  - Change 8 yards to feet.
  - Examples: 8 [×] 3 [=]
  - Display: 24
  - (1 yd = 3 ft.)
  - So, 8 yd = 24 ft

Use the [INT÷] or [×] keys on your calculator to complete the table.

| | | | 1 ft = 12 in. | 1 yd = 3 ft | 1 mi = 1,760 yd |
| | | | | 1 yd = 36 in. | 1 mi = 5,280 ft |

	Length	Change to	Write multiply or divide.	Copy the display.	Write answer with units.
1.	5 ft	in.	multiply	60	60 in.
2.	5 ft	yd	divide	1 2	1 yd, 2 ft
3.	43 ft	yd	divide	14 1	14 yd, 1 ft
4.	2 mi	yd	multiply	3520	3,520 yd
5.	10,000 ft	mi	divide	1 4720	1 mi, 4,720 ft
6.	3 mi	yd	multiply	5280	5,280 yd
7.	2,000 yd	mi	divide	1 240	1 mi, 240 yd
8.	444 in.	ft	divide	37 0	37 ft

Circle which measure is more. Then tell why.

9. (5 ft 8 in.) or 58 in.
   58 in. is 4 ft 10 in.

10. (50 yd) or 100 ft
    50 yd is 150 ft

11. 11 yd 2 ft or (36 ft)
    36 ft is 12 yd

12. 1 mi or (1795 yd)
    1795 yd is 1 mi 35 yd

Use with pages 390–391.

Technology Master 30
Using a Calculator to Find the Products of Fractions, Mixed Numbers, and Whole Numbers

Suggested Technology: Calculator—Math Explorer or equivalent

You can use the [/], [×], [UNIT] and [=] keys to multiply a fraction or mixed number by a whole number on your calculator. Use rounding to estimate the product first. Use the [Ab/c] and/or the [SIMP] key to simplify your answers.

Examples	Estimate	Press	Display
$\frac{4}{7} \times 19$	Round $\frac{4}{7}$ to $\frac{1}{2}$; $\frac{1}{2} \times 20 = 10$	4 [/] 7 [×] 19 [=] [Ab/c]	76/7 10u6/7

The estimate 10 is close to $10\frac{6}{7}$.

| $1\frac{7}{8} \times 6$ | Round $1\frac{7}{8}$ to 2; $2 \times 6 = 12$ | 1 [UNIT] 7 [/] 8 [×] 6 [=] [Ab/c] [SIMP] [=] | 90/8 11u2/8 11u1/4 |

The estimate 12 is close to $11\frac{1}{4}$.

Estimate each product. Then use your calculator to find the exact product in simplest form.

1. $\frac{4}{5} \times 18$ $1 \times 18 = 18$ $14\frac{2}{5}$
2. $1\frac{5}{8} \times 9$ $1\frac{1}{2} \times 10 = 15$ $14\frac{5}{8}$
3. $\frac{5}{6} \times 25$ $1 \times 25 = 25$ $20\frac{5}{6}$
4. $\frac{4}{9} \times 28$ $\frac{1}{2} \times 28 = 14$ $12\frac{4}{9}$
5. $1\frac{3}{8} \times 33$ $1\frac{1}{2} \times 32 = 48$ $45\frac{3}{8}$
6. $\frac{5}{6} \times 43$ $1 \times 43 = 43$ $35\frac{5}{6}$
7. $\frac{3}{11} \times 16$ $\frac{1}{4} \times 16 = 4$ $4\frac{4}{11}$
8. $3\frac{7}{8} \times 6$ $4 \times 6 = 24$ $23\frac{1}{4}$

Answers may vary.

Use with pages 407–408.

Technology Master 31
Using a Calculator to Multiply Whole Numbers by Fractions

Suggested Technology: Calculator—Math Explorer or equivalent

Use the [/], [×], and [=] keys to multiply whole numbers by fractions. You can use the [F↔D] key to change the product to a decimal.

The circle graph shows the production of about 290 million metric tons of wheat in four top-producing countries of the world.

How many metric tons of wheat were produced in the United States?

Press	Display
23 [/] 100 [×] 290	6670/100
[Ab/c]	66u70/100
[F↔D]	66.7

World Wheat Production Among Top 4 Countries

- Canada $\frac{1}{10}$
- India $\frac{7}{20}$
- United States $\frac{23}{100}$
- Former Soviet Union $\frac{31}{100}$

The United States produced about 66.7 million tons of wheat.

Use your calculator to solve each problem. Write each answer in decimal form.

1. How many metric tons of wheat were produced in India?   **101.5 million**
2. How many metric tons of wheat were produced in the former Soviet Union?   **89.9 million**
3. How many metric tons of wheat were produced in Canada?   **29 million**
4. How many more tons of wheat were produced in India than in the United States?   **34.8 million**
5. How many tons of wheat were produced in the United States and Canada?   **95.7 million**

Use with pages 420–421.

Technology Master 32
Using a Calculator to Multiply Whole Numbers and Mixed Numbers

Suggested Technology: Calculator—Math Explorer or equivalent

Use the [×], [UNIT], [/], and [=] keys to multiply whole and mixed numbers. Use the [Ab/c] key to convert improper fractions to whole or mixed numbers.

This is Frank's favorite brownie recipe.

How many cups of sugar would Frank need if he increased the recipe 6 times?

Press	Display
6 [×] 2 [UNIT] 1 [/] 2 [=]	30/2
[Ab/c]	15

Frank would need 15 cups of sugar.

Frank's Fudge Brownies
- $2\frac{1}{2}$ cups sugar
- $1\frac{2}{3}$ cups margarine
- 5 (1-oz) squares chocolate
- 4 large eggs
- $1\frac{3}{4}$ cups all-purpose flour
- $1\frac{1}{3}$ cups chopped nuts
- $\frac{1}{2}$ cup milk
- $1\frac{1}{4}$ tsp vanilla extract

Use your calculator and the recipe above to solve the following problems.

How many cups of margarine would Frank need if he increased the recipe 5 times?   **$8\frac{1}{3}$ cups**

How many cups of all-purpose flour would Frank need if he increased the recipe 8 times?   **14 cups**

How many teaspoons of vanilla extract would Frank need if he increased the recipe 5 times?   **$6\frac{1}{4}$ tsp**

How many cups of chopped nuts would Frank need if he increased the recipe 3 times?   **4 cups**

How many squares of chocolate would Frank need if he increased the recipe $2\frac{1}{2}$ times?   **$12\frac{1}{2}$ squares**

If this recipe makes 4 dozen brownies, what would you need to multiply the amount of each ingredient by to make 6 dozen brownies?   **Multiply by $1\frac{1}{2}$**

Use with pages 422–423.

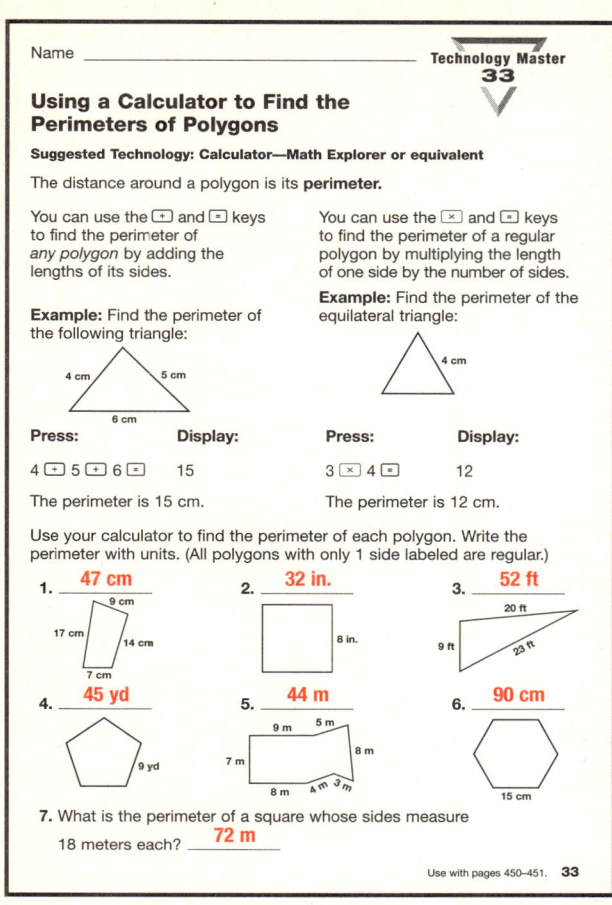

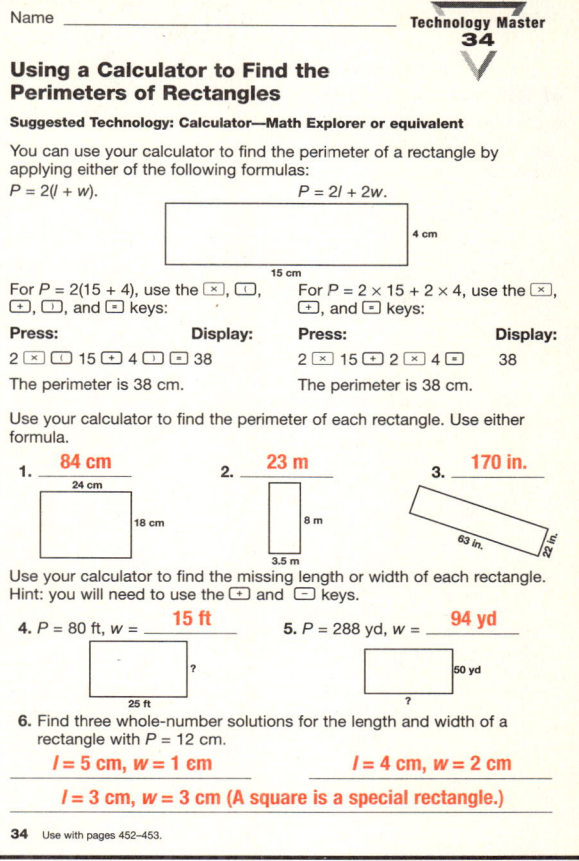

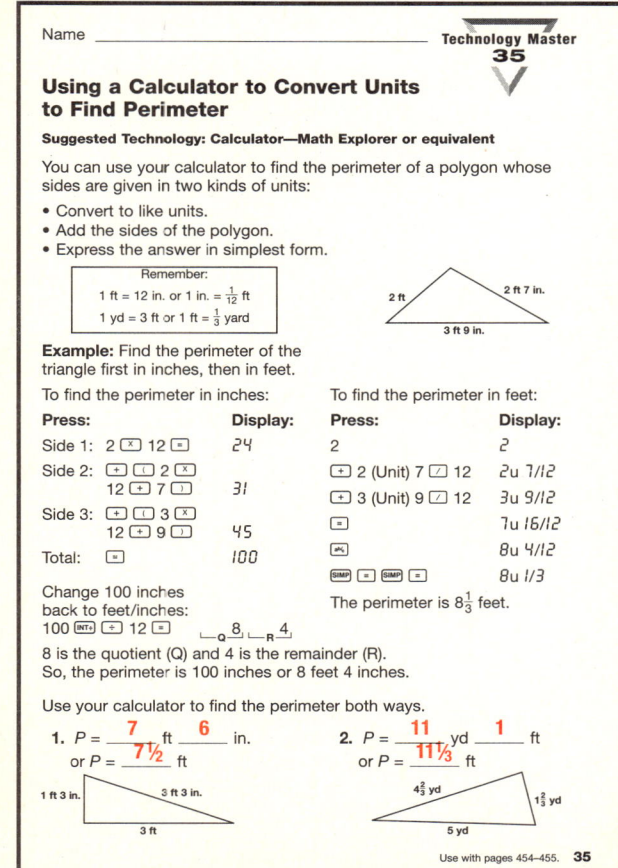

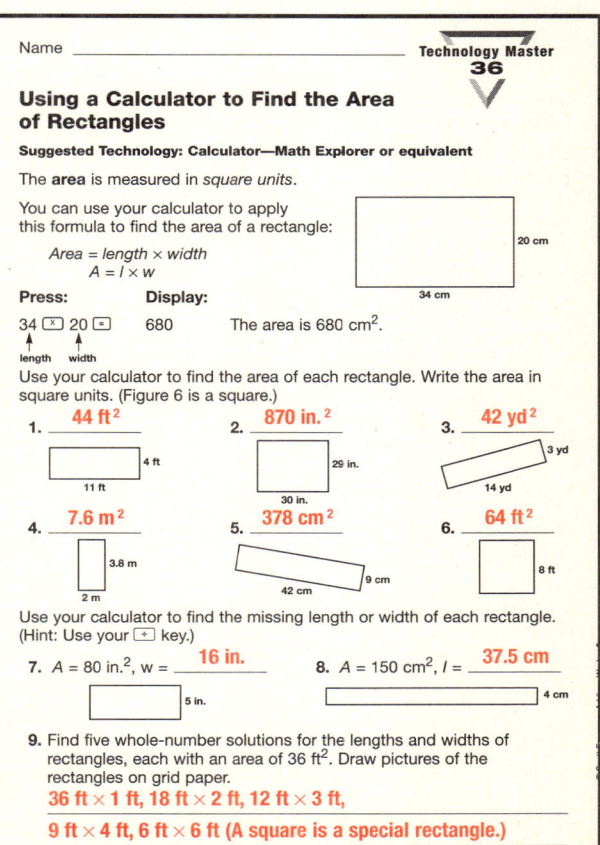

Name _____   Technology Master 37

Using a Calculator to Find Area of Triangles

Suggested Technology: Calculator—Math Explorer or equivalent

You can use your calculator to apply this formula to find the area of a triangle:

Count the units of the height.
Count the units of the base.

Area = $\frac{1}{2}$ (base × height)
$A = \frac{1}{2}(b \times h)$ or $A = \frac{1}{2} \times b \times h$

Example: Find the area of the triangle in square units.

Press: Display:
1 / 2 × 9 × 6 =   27   The area is 27 units².
 ↑   ↑
base height

Use your calculator to find the area of each triangle. Write the area in square units.

1. **12 units²** 2. **20 ft²** 3. **189 in²**

4. Use your calculator to find the area of each face and of the base of this square pyramid. Then find the total area. (Hint: A square pyramid has 4 faces and a base.)

Each face: ½ × 3 × 8 = 12;   **4 faces:** 4 × 12 = 48;
square base: 3 × 3 = 9;   **total area: 57 cm²**

Use with pages 466–467. 37

Name _____   Technology Master 38

Using a Calculator to Find the Area of Parallelograms

Suggested Technology: Calculator—Math Explorer or equivalent

You can use your calculator to apply this formula to find the area of a parallelogram:

Count the units of the height.
Count the units of the base.

Area = base × height
$A = b \times h$

Example: Find the area in square units:

Press: Display:
8 × 6 =   48   The area is 48 units².
↑ ↑
base height

Use your calculator to find the area of each parallelogram. Write the area in square units.

1. **16 units²** 2. **9 units²** 3. **15 units²**

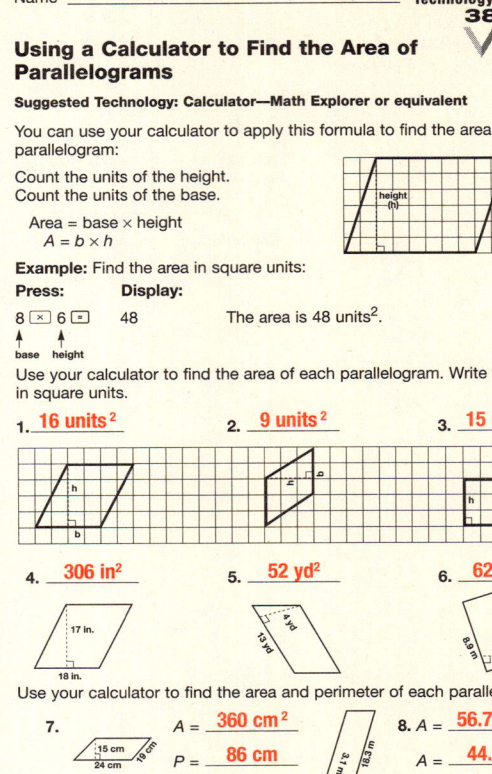

4. **306 in²** 5. **52 yd²** 6. **62.3 m²**

Use your calculator to find the area and perimeter of each parallelogram.

7. A = **360 cm²**   8. A = **56.73 m²**
    P = **86 cm**   A = **44.6 m**

38 Use with pages 470–471.

Name _____   Technology Master 39

Using a Calculator to Explore Circumference

Suggested Technology: Calculator—Math Explorer or equivalent

The distance around a circle is its **circumference**. The circumference is about 3 times longer than the diameter and is measured in *units*. You can use a calculator to apply this formula to find the circumference of a circle.

Circumference = π × diameter or π × 2 × radius
$C = \pi d$ $\pi \approx 3.14$ $C = \pi \times 2r$

The calculator uses a more precise decimal for π. Press the π key to see it! Use the FIX key to fix π to a certain number of decimal places.

Example: Find the circumference of a circle with a diameter of 8 cm. Solve the problem 3 ways to see how the answers differ.

Use the π key: Round π to hundredths: Use π ≈ 3.14:
Press: Display: Press: Display: Press: Display:
π   3.1415927   FIX 2 π 3.14   3 . 14   3.14
× 8 = 25.132741 × 8 =   25.13   × 8 =   25.12
↑
diameter
The circumference is about 25 cm.

Use your calculator to find the circumference 3 ways.

Diameter or Radius	Use π key	Use FIX 2 π keys	Use 3.14
1. d = 10 m	31.415927 m	31.42 m	31.4 m
2. r = 6 in.	37.699112 in.	37.70 in.	37.68 in.
3. d = 15 ft	47.12389 ft	47.12 ft	47.1 ft
4. r = 9 yd	56.548668 yd	56.55 yd	56.52 yd
5. d = 22 cm	69.115038 cm	69.12 cm	69.08 cm
6. r = 13 m	81.681409 m	81.68 m	81.64 m

Use with pages 476–477. 39

Name _____   Technology Master 40

Using a Calculator to Find Surface Area

Suggested Technology: Calculator—Math Explorer or equivalent

The **surface area** of any solid is equal to the sum of the areas of all of its faces. Surface area is measured in *square units*.

This is the formula for the surface area of any rectangular prism:

Surface area = (2 × front area)
             + (2 × side area)
             + (2 × top area)
             = total area of faces

You can use the memory keys M+ and MR on your calculator to find surface area. The M+ key adds a number to the memory. The MR key displays the contents of the memory.

Press   Display
2 × 5 × 6 = M+   60
2 × 3 × 6 = M+   36
2 × 3 × 5 = M+   30
MR   126

The surface area is 126 m².

Use your calculator to find the surface area of each rectangular prism.

1. Surface area = **268 ft²**
2. Surface area = **1,734 in²**
3. Surface area = **790 m²**
4. Surface area = **3,434 cm²**

5. Find the width of this solid if the surface area is 268 m². **8 m**

6. Show how to find the surface area of one of the solids above using the parentheses keys (and) instead of the memory keys.

For Problem 1, press
(2 × 4 × 11) + (2 × 4 × 6) +
(2 × 6 × 11) = 268

40 Use with pages 494–495.

Technology Master 41

Using a Calculator to Explore Ounces, Pounds, and Tons

Suggested Technology: Calculator—Math Explorer or equivalent

- When changing larger units to smaller units, *multiply*. Use the ☒ and ☐ keys.

Example	Press	Display
5 T = ___ lb	5 ☒ 2000 ☐	10000	5 T = 10,000 lb

Remember: 1 T = 2,000 lb

- When changing smaller units to larger units, divide. Use the INT÷ and ☐ keys. The number above the Q is the quotient. The number above the R is the remainder.

Example	Press	Display
43 oz = ___ lb	43 INT÷ 16 ☐	2 11	43 oz = 2 lb 11 oz

Remember: 1 lb = 16 oz

Use your calculator and the measurement facts above to complete the problems. Circle ☒ ___ or INT÷ ___ , then fill in the blank. Problem 1 has been done for you.

1. 9 lb ⊗☒ 16 = 144 oz
2. 14,000 lb ⊗INT÷ **2,000** = **7** T
3. 18 T ⊗☒ **2,000** = **36,000** lb
4. 125 oz ⊗INT÷ **16** = **7** lb **13** oz
5. 1,000 oz ⊗INT÷ **16** = **62** lb **8** oz
6. 54,321 lb ⊗INT÷ **2,000** = **27** T **321** lb
7. Find 1 T = **32,000** oz. How did you get your answer?
   Multiply 2,000 lb times 16 oz.

Use your calculator to convert each pair of measurements to the same unit. Then write <, >, or = in each ○.

8. 6 lb **>** 72 oz
   96 oz **>** 72 oz

9. 5 T **<** 15,000 lb
   10,000 lb **<** 15,000 lb

Use with pages 500–501. **41**

Technology Master 42

Using a Calculator to Find Volume

Suggested Technology: Calculator—Math Explorer or equivalent

The **volume** of a solid is the number of *cubic units* it contains. You can find the volume of a rectangular prism by using a formula and your calculator.

Example Volume = length × width × height
$V = l \times w \times h$
$V = 5 \text{ ft} \times 4 \text{ ft} \times 3 \text{ ft}$

Press	Display
5 ☒ 4 ☒ 3 ☐	60

The volume is 60 ft³. ← cubic units

Use your calculator to find the volume of each rectangular prism.

1. 12 in. / 6 in. / 15 in.
   V = **1,080 in³**

2. 22 cm / 20 cm / 59 cm
   V = **25,960 cm³**

3. 6 m / 3.5 m / 20 m
   V = **420 m³**

4. 13 ft / 13 ft / 13 ft
   V = **2,197 ft³**

Now find the volume of these solids.

5. 98 cm / 112 cm / 3 cm
   V = **32,928 cm³**

6.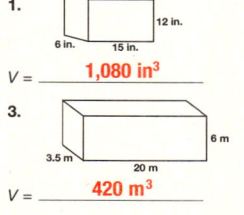
   V = **495 m³**

Find the surface area of the solids in Problems 1–4 above.

1. (2 × 12 × 15) + (2 × 6 × 12) + (2 × 6 × 15) = 684 in²
2. (2 × 20 × 59) + (2 × 20 × 22) + (2 × 22 × 59) = 5,836 cm²
3. (2 × 20 × 6) + (2 × 3.5 × 6) + (2 × 3.5 × 20) = 422 m²
4. 6 × 13 × 13 = 1,014 ft²

42 Use with pages 508–509.

Technology Master 43

Using a Calculator to Find Measurements for a Scale Drawing

Suggested Technology: Calculator—Math Explorer or equivalent

Use the scale drawing and your calculator to determine the actual measurements of the rooms in this house. Each square on the grid paper is 20 inches by 20 inches. Give each room's length and width in inches and then in feet and inches.

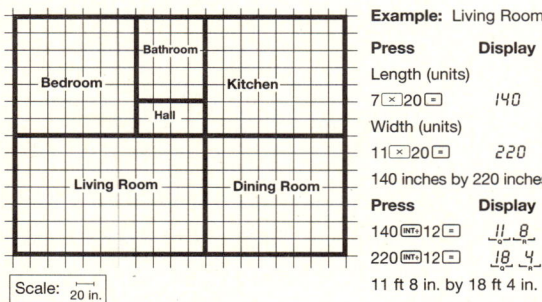

Example: Living Room

Press	Display
Length (units)	
7 ☒ 20 ☐	140
Width (units)	
11 ☒ 20 ☐	220

140 inches by 220 inches

Press	Display
140 INT÷ 12 ☐	11 8
220 INT÷ 12 ☐	18 4

11 ft 8 in. by 18 ft 4 in.

Scale: 20 in.

Room	Inches	Feet and Inches
Living Room	140 in. by 220 in.	11 ft 8 in. by 18 ft 4 in.
Dining Room	**160 in. by 140 in.**	**13 ft 4 in. by 11 ft 8 in.**
Bedroom	**140 in. by 140 in.**	**11 ft 8 in. by 11 ft 8 in.**
Bathroom	**100 in. by 80 in.**	**8 ft 4 in. by 6 ft 8 in.**
Kitchen	**160 in. by 140 in.**	**13 ft 4 in. by 11 ft 8 in.**
Hall	**80 in. by 40 in.**	**6 ft 8 in. by 3 ft 4 in.**
Outside Walls	**380 in. by 280 in.**	**31 ft 8 in. by 23 ft 4 in.**

Use with pages 536–537. **43**

Technology Master 44

Using a Calculator to Find the Percent of a Number

Suggested Technology: Calculator—Math Explorer or equivalent

Discount Warehouse

10-speed Bike $159.00 Sale 15% off	Space Watches $49.95 Any style 20% off	CD Players $89.00 Special 25% off
Comedy Videos $18.00 Discounted 33%	Headphones $34.75 Save 20%	CD Caddy $37.50 Super Sale—10% off

You can use your calculator to find the discount and sale price.

Example
What is the discount and sale price of a space watch?

	Press	Display	Amount
Discount →	49.95 ☒ 20 % ☐	9.99	$9.99
Sale Price →	49.95 ☐ 9.99 ☐	39.96	$39.96
	Original price Discount		

Discount is $9.99. Sale price is $36.96.

1. How much do you save when you buy the CD player on sale?
   89 × 25% = $22.25

2. What is the amount of discount on the 10-speed bike?
   159 × 15% = $23.85

3. What is the sale price of the CD Caddy?
   37.50 × 10% = 3.75; 37.50 − 3.75 = $33.75

4. How much money do you pay for a set of headphones on sale?
   34.75 × 20% = 6.95; 34.75 − 6.95 = $27.80

5. How much will it cost to buy 4 comedy videos on sale?
   4 × 18 = 72; 72 × 33% = 23.76; 72 − 23.76 = $48.24

6. What is the total cost of a 10-speed bike on sale with 6% sales tax added to it?
   159 × 15% = 23.85; 159 − 23.85 = 135.15;
   135.15 × 6% = 8.109; 135.15 + 8.11 = $143.26

44 Use with pages 542–543.